ANYONE
CAN
MAKE
BIG
MONEY
BUYING
ART

ALSO BY MORTON SHULMAN

Anyone Can Make a Million
Anyone Can Still Make a Million
The Billion Dollar Windfall

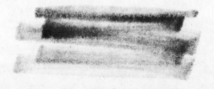

ANYONE CAN MAKE BIG MONEY BUYING ART

MORTON SHULMAN

MACMILLAN PUBLISHING CO., INC.
NEW YORK

Macmillan Publishing Co., Inc.
866 Third Avenue, New York, N.Y. 10022

Library of Congress Cataloging in Publication Data
Shulman, Morton.
Anyone can make big money buying art.
Includes index.
1. Art as an investment.   I. Title.
N8600.S55   332.6′78   77–834
ISBN 0–02–610560–8

First Printing 1977

Printed in the United States of America

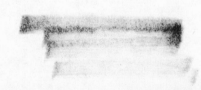

CONTENTS

ANYONE
CAN
MAKE
BIG
MONEY
BUYING
ART

I

INTRODUCTION

In 1953 I made my first investment in art—a little snuffbox which cost me $150. Today that snuffbox is worth $15,000. My second purchase was a lithograph by Vlaminck for $100, whose current value is $8,000. These price rises are not extraordinary—Chinese vases which sold for $300 eight years ago can bring $50,000 today, silver worth $100 in 1970 will easily bring $2,000, and a clock sold in a New York shop for $5,000 in 1955 has since been resold for $160,000. So it is not surprising that I have made a fortune in art and so have many of my friends.

What *is* surprising is the fact that, despite the tremendous price increases, great opportunities for investment remain. There are many fields of art which have been passed over by the boom and inflation, and they in turn will bound up in price in the next few years. In this book I will try to guide you to those fields and give you the kind of advice that will enable you to both enjoy and invest simultaneously—just as I have done.

The first thing that should be said is that you don't have to be rich to make money in the art market. You don't even need a big lump sum to begin, as you would in the stock market. If you have $500 to spend, you're in a position to start today. With that sum, profitable buys can be made

3

in enamel, Russian silver, old paintings, rose quartz, old glass, antiquities, or a dozen other fields. It's really very easy. The key words—the things that you must learn to exploit—are beauty and inflation.

Fine art and art objects are perhaps the only investment that will give you as much pleasure as profit. A beautiful painting, a finely wrought stone carving, an unusual work of folk art—these things have a value above and beyond their actual worth. The element of taste, or aesthetic pleasure, or desire—call it what you will—helps to determine what you, or anyone else, is willing to pay for a work of art: aesthetics are as important as economics in understanding the art market.

Since the first civilization, man has always wanted to possess lovely things to admire and wonder at and to share his pleasure with his friends. Even in times and in countries where large numbers of the population were starving, there have always been a few wealthy citizens, a few patrons of the arts, who had the funds and the time to collect the beautiful objects that were available. The phenomenon of the public museum, a place where art can be "owned" and shared by the entire population, is recent, but even today public galleries and museums collect only a small part of the available treasures; most are still in private hands.

So the goods are still there. The question is, can you get at them? And the answer, for the most part, is yes. It must be said that in recent decades a new trend has appeared: nations are attempting to protect their national treasures by refusing to allow their export; and following the smuggling out of important pieces, strenuous efforts have been made to get them back. Up to the Second World War there were no such restrictions, but a wave of nationalism swept Europe and Asia after 1945 and country after country became increasingly resentful toward the rich individuals and nations who were stripping them of their heritage. The problem was summed up by a British Member of Parliament, Raymond Fletcher, in a debate in the House of Commons in July 1976: "If we make it a principle that we sell everything to the United States that is saleable, at what point do we sell the Palace of Westminster to Disneyland?" This attitude resulted in a series of laws preventing the export of important art works from every European nation and most Asian and Latin American ones. Even Canada has now passed a restrictive law hindering the sale of anything over one hundred years old to those rich Americans.

As a result of this kind of legislation, it may very well be that the days of accumulating great collections—the days of an Andrew Mellon or a J. P. Morgan—have come to an end. But one thing is certain: the art market is still wide open, and the ordinary small investor will continue to be able to accumulate beautiful and rewarding collections— the rewards being both aesthetic and financial. The difference between the Mellons and the ordinary investor is that extremely valuable objects are watched and protected by foreign governments, but small treasures—those worth only a few hundred dollars—are not restricted and can

5

be freely bought and sold at great profit. I know, because I have done it, and the purpose of this book is to show how any of you can do the same.

Why Art Is the Best Investment

Throughout my life I have had a great weakness for beautiful things, and over the last thirty years I have been fortunate enough to be able to acquire a large number of unusual and rare art objects. Oddly enough I didn't start by buying any of these as an investment—I bought them because they were beautiful, and I wanted them—but they have ended up giving a greater financial gain than the best stock or bond I ever owned.

I bought my first painting in 1953. I had made a great deal of money in the stock market, and an older friend suggested I purchase some "name" art to grace my home. I walked into the Laing Gallery in Toronto and asked Blair Laing to show me any Impressionist paintings he had in stock. He showed me a Dufy, a Utrillo, and a Rouault, and I blithely wrote a check for $14,000 and happily walked out. In 1959 I resold those three paintings at auction at Parke Bernet for $35,000 and bought a new home with the proceeds. Today they would be worth about $100,000. Let me stress that this was blind luck and is hardly a model to follow.

When the word "art" is mentioned most people think of paintings, but paintings represent only a small segment of the art market—and not even the most profitable segment, at that. My own biggest coup was in the watch field: a pair of automata watches whose backs are covered with split pearls and whose fronts show two musicians who play in time with the music the watches play when they strike the hour (Figure 1). Automata watches made in pairs are extremely rare, and this pair may be unique. I found them in a Hong Kong curio shop in 1958—not really an odd place for such a discovery. Toward the end of the eighteenth century a ready market developed in China for clocks and watches with moving parts, and several English dealers established offices in Canton to distribute these objects. This pair went to China about 1790 and remained there in private hands until 1949. After the communist takeover that year many wealthy Chinese fled in haste to Hong Kong, and because of the chaos and difficulty in transportation they were only able to carry with them valuables that were both small and precious. When I bought them they cost me $250. I sold them ten years later for $2,500, and the New York dealer who bought them from me resold them for $60,000 in 1976. Most important, the huge increase in value far outpaces the inflation the dollar has seen since 1958—which makes these watches one of the best hedges against inflation I know of.

Inflation has been the scourge of the free world for the past twenty years. It has been in large part responsible for the dissension, rising prices, and labor unrest that have plagued the United States and Canada since 1965, but it has produced a tremendous windfall for almost everyone involved in the art world, be they dealers or collectors. The reason for this windfall is very simple. Art has increased in price far faster than the dollar has lost its buying power because art is one of the few things that people can count on as a way of protecting capital. The German inflation of the 1920's illustrated this very well. In 1923 when the mark was worth 25¢ a small Rembrandt portrait was sold for 30,000 marks—in 1925 the mark had sunk to 1,000 to the dollar and the portrait was resold for 10,000,000 marks. In 1926 as the mark collapsed even further the same portrait was auctioned in Berlin for 45,000,000,000 marks!

There are other things whose intrinsic value is equally stable, land being the perfect example, but most of these are subject to governmental interference, taxation, or confiscation. In fact, people who attempted to protect themselves against inflation by buying cheap land in Canada received a rude shock in May 1974, when the Ontario government introduced a land speculation tax which resulted in the taking away of 80 percent of all apparent profits—with an especially heavy tax on Americans and other foreigners. Actually, most of these were only paper profits resulting from the loss of value of the dollar. The result was that a person who bought a piece of land as an inflationary hedge in 1973 and paid $50,000 for it saw its value go to $65,000 three years later, purely as a result of inflation. But if he attempted to sell that land the government would tax away most of the $15,000 "profit," and the final result would be that the investor would have slipped behind in real buying power.

Governments will tax whatever they feel will yield substantial funds, but no government anywhere has figured out how to tax art work efficiently. It is easy to tell if someone has sold a piece of land because the transaction goes through the registry office, but it is obviously impossible in a democratic system to tell if an individual has bought or sold a watch. Governments try, of course: many countries have instituted a capital gains tax, but because of the difficulty of collection and the ease of concealment most countries have kept the tax relatively low, and nowhere does it exceed 25 percent. The result is that in many ways art is the most protected investment possible.

It is also one of the surest to appreciate in value. Since a work of art is relatively immune to inflation, it will become more and more valuable as inflation continues. And it will continue. Economists speak of inflation as though it is a mysterious event but it is a simple matter and one which has been repeated countless times through history. Politicians seek popularity by promising things to the voting public—higher pensions, broader highways, increased mothers' allowances, subsidized art, or a new post office—and Mr. Average Public responds by giving the politicians his vote. Once the politicians are in office they realize the promises must be paid for, but they also realize that raising taxes to pay for them is the surest way to lose votes. So political parties of every stripe have taken the easy way out—the printing of paper money. Every year governments spend more money than they take in and they make up the difference by printing more paper, the end result being that every year that paper buys less and less.

There is no question that this process will continue and

accelerate, and if the history of other countries is any guide, the rate of inflation will increase to somewhere over 20 percent per annum by 1982. At the same time, a 20-percent inflation rate will undoubtedly be balanced by a 30- to 50-percent rise in the value of art works, so the judicious purchaser of art will unquestionably do well financially in the next few years.

Some investors will question this assertion, and will hesitate to buy because of the tremendous price rises we have seen throughout the art field in recent years. Hasn't art become inflated in price too? they will ask. It is a fact that the price of most art today is actually lower than it was sixty years ago in terms of a constant currency. In 1963, Gerald Reitlinger wrote a classic analysis of the rise and fall of art prices since 1750 which he called *The Economics of Taste* (Barrie & Rockliff, London), in which he pointed out:

Disturbing as it may be to those who know of art pieces only through newspaper headlines, the value of several of the dearest sorts of objets d'art has fallen in the present century quite heavily. "Four thousand guineas for a commode," one reads in a headline one-half inch high, but they were paying four thousand guineas for a commode a hundred years ago. "Australia reached in sixty-five days" would not be less up-to-date news. In terms of actual purchasing power, the highest price-levels which are achieved today for French furniture and objets d'art of the eighteenth century are not a fraction of what they were fifty and even eighty-five years ago. The sum of £25,000, the equivalent of not more than £4,200 in 1912, and perhaps even less in 1878, is an enormous price in the early 1960s for the most splendid piece of English or French furniture. Yet it is not nearly enough to buy the sloppiest and most perfunctory of the few still available oil sketches of Renoir and Cézanne. It is barely sufficient to buy even the most mindless of abstract paintings that happens to have the right signature or label.

It is fascinating to see how objects have jumped in price since Reitlinger completed his book in 1963. He thought that Renoir was relatively overpriced then, yet by 1968 Renoir's work had doubled again and there was still lots of room for the new investor to make money. I proved it by purchasing an etching by Renoir that very year.

There are very few Renoir etchings. I bought one, dated 1907, from Brentano's art shop in New York for $450 (Figure 2). At that time that appeared to be a horrendous price, but since then the cost of etchings by modern artists has soared to apparently ridiculous levels— in fact an etching from a small edition by Cézanne, Chagall, or Léger can now sell for $10,000 or $15,000. In my opinion they are grossly overpriced—after all, if there are fifty or one hundred exactly the same, why should this be worth more than a photographically reproduced print? However, the fact remains that an exact copy of my etching sold this year at auction for $6,500, and if I chose to sell mine (my wife loves it, however, and won't let me sell it!) I would be able to realize a tremendous profit.

It's purely and simply a result of inflation, and although the *buying* price was inflated, the *selling* price would be even more so. Don't let the absurd prices paid for Impressionist art discourage you, though. One of the reasons for the high price tags is also the reason you can still find bargains in the art market: namely, the fluctuations of taste and fashion. This is where the aesthetics of the art market influence the economics. For the works of the Impressionist painters are now at the height of their vogue: they are fashionable, as well as beautiful, and everyone wants them. But there are other art objects, no less beautiful, that have not yet become status symbols; and these represent excellent value as an investment. Some, like Japanese ivory carvings, are even cheaper than they were two generations ago. In 1887, in Osaka, Sawiki Masaduzu carved a small box that looks like an ivory bag of one hundred mice (Figure 3). In 1893, Edgar McDonough Esq. of Toronto purchased it from Ikeda Antiques in Kyoto. I bought it in 1956 from Wolfson Antiques for $300. Today because of inflation it would sell for ten times that figure, and yet it still has lots of room to go up in price.

If you realize that in that same eleven-year period inflation has reduced the buying power of the dollar by half, there is an actual profit here of 500 percent. And there are countless other areas where the price tags are not nearly as high as we imagine—especially in contrast to what they once were. Here, for example, are prices for similar pieces of Renaissance crystal jewelry taken from London auctions:

1823	£630	1934	£880
1861	£496	1943	£340
1893	£2,800	1957	£2,100
1910	£600	1963	£840
1924	£6,000		

Don't be fooled by our inflation. There's still room for profit. As New York art dealer Sam Salz put it, "It's not the pictures that aren't worth the money. It's the money that isn't worth the money anymore."* And the pictures are going to be worth more and more in the months ahead, if the word of experts is anything to go by. In November 1976 a meeting was held in New York of the world's leading dealers and collectors and it was their opinion that although art had been overpriced in the past that stage was now over and there was now a solid basis for further early and substantial advances. They agreed that there is now a tremendous inflow of art investment money into the New York market; it comes particularly from Italy and England where investors are seeking to avoid the dangers of holding lira or pounds. Much of that currency is being turned into art and a great new price surge is about to begin.

* Milton Esterow, *The Art Stealers* (revised edition), Macmillan Publishing Co., Inc., New York, 1973.

II

WHAT

TO

BUY

You've just decided that the art market makes sense to you as an investor. You love beautiful things and want to collect them; you're looking for a solid, inflation-proof investment. But what should you buy? Old masters' drawings? Eighteenth-century silver? Pre-Columbian sculpture? Contemporary lithographs? Does it matter?

It certainly does. The art market is in some ways like the stock market. It is no more sensible to buy just any piece of art than it would be to buy just any stock. The first decision you must make is what field you wish to enter, since there are literally dozens of different areas ranging from paperweights to violins. Here your individual taste should always govern your choice—the inlaid silver that I find exquisite may leave you cold, while I find someone else's passion for Bokhara rugs incomprehensible. The first rule in buying art for investment is the same as buying art for decoration: *buy items that turn you on.* If you don't get pleasure from looking at them you are missing out on a very large dividend. And furthermore, if *you*

14

don't like a work of art that you've bought, you can't possibly be sure of its appeal for others—which, after all, will determine its resale value.

One thing you should be aware of is that *real profits* in the art market—the "big money" of our title—are almost all medium- or long-term profits, with a minimum hold of one year. Rarely do you have the experience, which I've frequently enjoyed in the stock market, of buying in the morning and selling profitably in the afternoon. But I have occasionally been able to buy something at auction only to have the underbidder—the person who dropped out of the bidding before I did—try to turn around and buy the same piece from me at a 10-percent markup.

And remember that the supply of valuable high-grade objects is drying up, so those that are available for sale gradually become more valuable. Quality is the single most important element in the acquisition of a work of art; it doesn't matter what price range of art you are buying into as long as you buy the best in your price range. In the dip in prices for Impressionist art in the early seventies, the second-rate paintings went down but the great Cézannes and Monets continued to sell at top prices.

A Big Investment or a Small One?

An important general rule in buying art is to avoid large objects because the difficulty involved in their transport lowers their resale value. One example is the clock in Figure 5. In the mid-nineteenth century, Europe went crazy over moving picture clocks. In this example, purchased from A La Vieille Russie in New York City, the windmill turns, the waterwheel turns, a train chugs across the background, and the boat rocks realistically. I paid $600 for it in 1957, but others like it have appreciated only modestly in recent years and today are still available for $2,000 or $3,000.

Another large object I bought that never really appreciated in value was a cast of Rodin's *The Kiss* made in the artist's studio by his pupil Barbedienne the year after Rodin's death. It is one of fifty copies and I got it at an auction at Parke Bernet twenty years ago for $1,600. It would probably bring in little more than twice that figure today because of its sixteen-inch height.

Big pieces of statuary like this, large clocks, suits of armor, and massive furniture are not only difficult to transport, they are difficult to display and maintain. The day of the spacious family house—fully staffed with numerous domestic servants—is over, and the demand for the kind of objects such houses used to contain has shrunk steadily over the years. As a result their prices have remained fairly static: you can buy a moving picture clock or a suit of armor for little more than you would have paid for it fifty years ago, but you won't get much more than that for it when you try to sell it. Big items are usually a bad investment—stay away from them.

Smaller objects, on the other hand, are portable: they can be easily guarded in a safe-deposit box or slipped into a pocket if you have to make a hasty exit. It's unlikely that any of us in the United States or Canada will face a revolution, but then the people in Portugal felt just as secure a few years ago. In any case, there is no question that thousands of wealthy Arabs, Iranians, Turks, Italians, and Chinese in various Asian countries consider that they may have to run in a hurry one of these days, and so they direct their investments away from land, local bonds, and large antiques and toward small gold objects, beautiful watches, elaborate snuffboxes, and ornate jewelry. It is this kind of demand that tends to push up the cost of small art objects on the international market.

The English representatives of the United Arab Emirates are always on the lookout for small jeweled cases, expensive "singing bird" boxes, or jeweled automata watches—the high price and small size of these objects make them so desirable.

One of my friends is a wealthy banker in Zurich who puts all his surplus funds into nineteenth-century Russian silver cigarette boxes. As he puts it, "My pieces are small, they are authentic, they are valuable and I don't have to worry about any government confiscating or taxing them."

This demand for small art objects has an interesting and unexpected dividend. You might think that, in the event that a revolution or other upheaval forces the quick sale of many small pieces, the resultant dumping of objects on the market would cause a fall in demand and therefore a decrease in value. Not so, for in the wake of such international convulsions, other wealthy groups across the world shiver a little and look for liquidity. The confiscation and sale of King Farouk's expensive baubles were followed within a year by a doubling in their price as they were grabbed up and locked away. So when you're making a decision about what to collect and buy, think small.

Singing birds are among the most beautiful and charming antiques that can be collected. These toys have been made for hundreds of years; Marie Antoinette kept several at Versailles. Ten years ago I bought one at Sotheby's for $50 (Figure 4). It dates from about one hundred years ago and is made of mother-of-pearl: when the slide at the side is pushed the lid lifts, the bird pops up and chirps a song while it flaps its wings, moves its beak, and turns back and forth. At the end of the song the bird goes back into the box and the lid closes automatically. The enameled bird box is brand-new and similar boxes are currently being made in Germany. They sell for about $300 and are certain to go way up in price over the next few years because their intrinsic value—based on the beauty of the enamel work and the musical but lifelike quality of the "bird's" song—will be enhanced by the fact that these are *really* limited editions.

Not all small items are safe investments. Anything breakable—however lovely—will be a problem to store, and if you're looking for quick profits, you should probably avoid purchases like the iridescent Syrian glass I purchased from Spinks of London in 1967 for $100 (Figure 6). It was made 2,000 years ago, and in view of its fragility it is a miracle it has survived. It was found in 1905 in a hoard in what is now Iraq. Antiquities are the only collecting field where prices have remained fairly stable, and today represent the best value of any art investment.

Glasses similar to this one can be purchased for about $250 today. It is their difficulty in *safe* portability that has prevented their soaring in price. On the other hand, if you have a safe storage place your piece must increase in value as other similar pieces are broken and yours becomes rarer.

Another thing to consider besides portability is storage-ability. Every dealer is aware of the trend in recent years away from displaying one's art collection. Traditionally the art collector would line his walls with his paintings and place other art objects in conspicuous display cabinets in his living room, but as a response to the hysterical time we live in, more and more collectors are hiding their expensive pieces in safe-deposit boxes—there is just too much risk of theft or malicious damage.

And this brings me back to size. Remember that it is a lot easier to store a watch than a statue, a small painting than a mural, a ring than a piece of furniture.

When making a collection for investment purposes always think of its safety. Are your pieces so large that when you go away on holiday they must remain at risk in your home, or are they small enough to be moved for safekeeping?

Something Old or Something New?

A good rule to follow in collecting art is to buy old pieces rather than recent works. Anything defined by the government as an antique can be imported duty free, and

19

this freedom to cross borders without cost increases an item's value. The U.S. government has defined as an antique any object over one hundred years old; back in 1944 when the Office of Price Administration exempted antiques from price controls it defined them this way:

(1) old objects such as furniture, tableware, household articles etc. (over 75 years old) which (2) tend to increase rather than decrease in value because of age; which (3) are purchased primarily because of their authenticity, age, rarity, style etc. rather than for their utility; and which (4) are commonly known and dealt in as antiques by the trade.

Change seventy-five years to one hundred and you have a pretty good guide to what to look for in art investment today.

What Not to Buy

If you really mean to make money—and find real values—in the art market, there are certain kinds of art to avoid entirely.

Ten years ago I wrote a book called *Anyone Can Make a Million*; it was primarily a guide to the stock market, but en passant I mentioned that modern art was a bad investment because most of it would have no resale value. The reaction from the art community was one of fury—I was denounced in the press and on television by numerous painters, sculptors, and other artists as a man with no taste and no knowledge of the subject, and I was told I should be seeking advice, not giving it. One artist was so enraged that he threatened to punch me out on a television show and I was forced to make a rather hasty and ungraceful flight from the station. I wasn't as lucky a few days later: I was attending a cocktail party and was shaking hands with my hostess when another infuriated artist came up, took one look, and let fly with a powerful right. I didn't know what hit me and as I scrambled off the floor my first thought was that there had been an earthquake!

Looking back, I can certainly understand their fury, for I am sure that, as a physician, I would have been just as angered if someone had suggested that a sick person was foolish going to a doctor and would do better going to a chiropractor. However, fortunately for my reputation as an investor, I find that many of those artists who were so voluble in 1966 have now disappeared from the art scene and have found easier ways to earn their livings; on those rare occasions when their paintings appear at auction the few bids are a fraction of the price the paintings were offered at a dozen years ago. Some, of course, still enjoy fine critical reputations and an excellent market for their work; but the hitch in purchasing modern art is that there are so many artists but so little room for success. When you think that in Rembrandt's time there were over one hundred other artists at work in his city, and when you realize how few of them are even remembered today, you have some idea of the problem. Out of the hundreds of modern artists, the work of only the occasional one will survive his own lifetime.

Obviously the trick is to pick that one, but I am just not

that smart and neither are you. Buying modern art as an investment is like buying stock in some "penny moose pasture" drilling prospect—the drill hole might find an ore body, but the prospect is extremely unlikely, and the overwhelming chance is that you will lose your money.

The exceptions appear very exciting, of course. In 1946, paintings by Jackson Pollock sold for $100. By 1953 their price had risen to $2,000, by 1960 to $25,000, and in 1973, one Pollock actually sold for $2,000,000. Of course, by comparison with old art that has passed the tests of time and changing taste, no modern painting is worth anything like that kind of money, and Pollock's prices have been pushed up to their stratospheric levels by clever promotion and a brilliant dealer. My prediction is that in future years Pollock's paintings will descend in price as precipitously as they rose.

Certainly many of his less well known contemporaries' works are already unsaleable, and although it is too soon to tell, Tom Wolfe has suggested in his book *The Painted Word* (Farrar, Straus & Giroux, New York, 1975) that, except for occasional museum buying "in the name of history," these wonders of modern art have never really appealed to the general public but only enjoyed an "in" vogue among a few willing critics and their tiny circle of wealthy admirers.

Those few living American artists who have been successful have seen their prices soar to levels that cannot be explained, justified, or sustained in a historical context. Thus a good Rauchenberg drawing will sell today for the same price as a Canaletto; I would guarantee that the Canaletto will have retained its value twenty years hence —but who would care to bet on the value then of the Rauchenberg? There is an instructive example to be found in the fate of Surrealist art, which was the victim of modern art's most recent boom-and-bust cycle. Four years ago paintings by Magritte or Ernst sold for tens of thousands of dollars, but today they are almost unsaleable.

What it boils down to in buying modern art is this: never buy it as an investment, but if you see something you like and it will give you pleasure, pay only for what that pleasure is worth. I have a dear friend whose husband has done very well in business; periodically she "invests" some of his money in modern art. She began by tastefully decorating the house with inexpensive prints and lithographs but ended up by being led down the garden path by a local dealer who persuaded her to buy modern limited edition lithographs for prices up to $12,000. Lithographs—in fact all graphics—are of course very much in fashion now; they are seen as an inexpensive way of acquiring the work of a contemporary artist. And that is precisely what is wrong with them as an investment: they are contemporary creations, and their *scarcity value* cannot develop in our lifetime—after all, we are investing for ourselves, not our grandchildren. At least I am. When I saw my friend's lithographs I realized to my horror that she had covered her walls with modern art which had cost her over $100,000 and which could be resold at only a fraction of that figure. When her husband woke up to what she had done the pleasures of ownership quickly disappeared. Now they both hate to look at her purchases.

Beware!

What about Limited Editions?

During the last decade and as a result of the upsurge in prices in almost every field of art, a new industry has sprung forth to satisfy the increasing demand for antiques, art, and beautiful things—the manufacture of so-called limited editions. The idea was originated by the owners of the Franklin Mint, who were the first to realize that affluent Americans would be happy to pay $25 or $50 each for attractive, well-designed coinlike medals when they were told that each of those medals was being issued in a limited number to commemorate a special event.

Following the fantastic financial success of the Franklin Mint, dozens of other companies have rushed to get into this gold mine, and now we have limited editions of coins, plates, ceramics, lithographs, and even of photographs. It is true that huge fortunes have been made in this field, but those fortunes were made not by the purchasers of the limited editions but by the sellers. Common sense should indicate that in this field, where the so-called limited editions are limited only by the ingenuity of their manufacturers, sooner rather than later the market will become satiated, the after market for these items will collapse, and the buyers will be stuck.

24

One of the leading firms in this field has a very interesting gimmick in which they run ads in various newspapers offering the public the chance to get in on a new series of limited edition coins only if they enroll by a certain date. As an experiment I had my secretary (I couldn't do this myself because my name might have been recognized) send in the coupon and her check one month after the deadline had expired, and I was considerably impressed when the company returned her check, saying she was too late because the subscription list had been closed. I was not quite so impressed the following week when she received a phone call from a company salesman saying that he was willing to make an exception in her case and would she please send the check in again.

If you are buying or subscribing to one of the limited editions because the object itself appeals to you, that is one thing; but if you are considering them as an investment the odds are impossible. Don't waste your money!

Of course, no rule would be a rule without an exception, and here the exception is a limited edition of a beautiful object, issued by some public institution or government body to commemorate a special occasion. A perfect example was the shipping by the Chinese government of a $100,000,000 collection of recent tomb finds of ancient objects to Europe and North America in 1974. The collection was put on exhibit for five weeks each in Paris, London, Toronto, and Washington. To commemorate the historic visit the fortunate gallery in each city made up to two hundred copies of the most beautiful object in the collection, the flying horse of Kangsi, and sold these numbered replicas for $500 each (Figure 7). At each of the four galleries the sculptures were snapped up within minutes of their going on sale and since then a number have changed hands at prices ranging between $600 and $1,000. If you read in your paper of a similar opportunity —grab it!

Fakes

Fakes are the ultimate bad investment. Obviously no one buys a forgery intentionally, but many people begin investing in fields that are full of fakes. These people are just asking to be cheated. When you're considering what to buy, stay away from fields and genres in which fakery is prevalent.

If you follow this rule religiously, you will beware of Judaica. I bought a lovely "antique" Judaic marriage ring (Figure 8) in New York in 1964 for $500—alas, it is a fake made in Portugal within the last decade. I also found a "nineteenth-century" pointer, used to follow the reading of the Torah, in a shop in Spain in 1973 (Figure 9). It appeared a great bargain at $125 until I discovered the factory in Madrid that was turning them out by the gross. (Actually as a modern piece it is still not bad value. It was made by hand and some day it will be an antique.)

The field of pre-Columbian art has been almost completely destroyed for the amateur collector by tens of thousands of fakes. Visitors to Mexico and Central and

South America are always surprised by the multitude of pre-Columbian objects offered at very reasonable prices. The authenticity of these objects is invariably guaranteed by an impressive certificate. But alas, both the object and the certificate are almost always of the same vintage. Or so I found when I bought a "Momil culture" bowl in Colombia.

The price *was* reasonable—only $65—but the object was not quite 1,000 years old. When I took it to the curator of my local museum he told me it had been made right in Bogotá two years earlier.

What it boils down to is that the fakes are exact copies of museum items, and sometimes even the experts can't tell which is the genuine article.

The investor should stay away from this field entirely.

Furniture and paintings are both very popular with investors and very much prey to forgery, because they are easy to copy. I will never forget my shock in 1971 when I was taken to the "Louis XIV period" factory just outside Rome. Artisans there carefully copied furniture from museum and catalog pictures while one floor down the "distressor" beat the same beautiful furniture with flat boards in order to age it artificially. There is little protection in the furniture field from the forger although experts claim they can tell the difference. For this reason a large investment in old furniture is pretty chancy. Certainly I wouldn't put my money there.

Fake paintings are legion and inasmuch as even experts in this field have often been fooled the amateur should beware. The story of Clifford Irving's friend de Hory is a classic—his phony Impressionists almost ruined that market; in Belgium Van Meegeren turned out dozens of "old masters" which he sold to Goering and other art experts, and in Toronto one art dealer hired a previously unsuccessful painter to turn out "Krieghoffs" by the dozen which he easily auctioned off through what was then Toronto's largest auction house. I'm embarrassed to admit that I was stung early in my buying by the same dealer, who for $400 sold me a small "Gainsborough" (Figure 10). It seemed like a good price, since the dealer was making me a special offer (Figure 11).

I happily hung the painting in my living room where it remained for several months until that horrible day when I saw in the paper that that particular dealer had been arrested for selling fake pictures. I rushed with the "Gainsborough" down to the Ontario Art Gallery where the curator sadly informed me that the picture had been completed within the last five years and unless Gainsborough was working from the spirit world it was unlikely to have been done by him.

There are other fields to stay away from:

Italy specializes not only in fake old furniture, but also in amazingly good fake Fabergé that is almost as beautiful as the original. These objects come from a "Fabergé" factory in Florence. Watch out for them.

Lebanon, until the recent civil war, turned out thousands of fake ancient and not-so-ancient gold and silver coins. Some were so good that the entire market for the item was destroyed. In Turkey the dealers went so far as to bury hoards of these "old" coins which they then allowed amateur archeologists to find at a dig. So stay away from antique and old coins.

Specialize

A most important rule in buying art is to specialize as soon as possible.

There are so many fields of art and so many subdivisions in each field that no individual can be expert in every area: the more you diversify the less likely you are to invest wisely. My own tastes have been far too catholic and as a result I have overpaid on many a purchase. When that happens it doesn't matter whether you've invested a hundred dollars or several thousand—the money is usually wasted if you don't know what you're doing. For instance, huge fortunes can be made in tapestries—but not by me. This is a highly specialized field requiring expert knowledge, and I can't tell a new tapestry from an old one. I innocently bought a brand-new piece in Belgium fifteen years ago for $300 (Figure 12). Today it is almost worth $300.

My enthusiasm for beautiful things, coupled with a lack of specialized knowledge, has led me astray far more expensively than that, however. Once my eye was caught by a perfect piece of jadeite worked into a contemporary Chinese carving. It was produced in Peking in 1974 and was chosen by the Chinese government as an example of their best jade. The price tag on this piece was $17,000, which is no bargain. Undeterred, however, I went back for more. From the same shop as the jadeite a piece of malachite, carved in much the same fashion, was shipped to Canada by the Chinese government as a sample of their finest work (Figure 13). They charged me $4,000 for the carving. I suspect that I will not profit from either of these purchases. The reason should have been apparent to me, but—dazzled as I was by the beauty of the stone and inexperienced as I was in this field of art—I simply didn't see it. What I never realized was that China has a vast supply of first-class jadeite and malachite, as well as a veritable army of expert stone-carvers; the Chinese can thus turn out an unlimited supply of pieces similar to the two I bought. Learn the lesson I *didn't* learn until it was too late: if there is no rarity value in a piece, a high price cannot be sustained for it. You may pay dearly for it, but you'll get very little more for it than you paid.

The great advantage of specializing in one field is that it is much easier to become an expert not only as to authenticity but also as to rarity and value. Of course whatever field you choose—whether it is sporting paintings or Oriental art or French porcelain—should not be too broad; just as a stamp collector will not collect *all* stamps, but will specialize in one country or one period, so the art collector should similarly limit himself.

Choosing Your Specialty

You need not set about specializing deliberately, from the outset. Start with a kind of object, or a period or a genre, that interests you; then let your inclinations guide you from there. I developed my specialty in automata watches—a specialty that offers a number of important lessons to the beginning collector—more by chance than by design. I began by collecting just watches, of which there are millions; then I began to focus more narrowly on handmade enameled repeaters of the eighteenth and nineteenth centuries, of which there are tens of thousands. Then, in 1954, I was strolling on New York's Fifth Avenue and glanced in the window of A La Vieille Russie, on the corner of Fifty-ninth Street. There in the window were some exquisite antique watches, part of a loan exhibition that the shop was putting on, and beside them were copies of the exhibit's catalog. I went in and bought a catalog for $2—and I fell in love forever with the fascinating pieces pictured in it. The catalog's introduction, by Professor Alfred Chapuis, goes part of the way toward explaining the spell cast over me by these automata:

These objects, intended for delight rather than for use, are the playthings of a subtle art and of superb craftsmanship. When seen as a collection, they appear a fairy garden which in its old-world grace and glitter represents a fascinating aspect of the skill of other days.

I didn't know it at the time, but the field I had suddenly chosen to specialize in fulfilled the most basic rules for the beginning art collector—rules you should note down and follow if you're serious about making money in the art market.

They were readily available. This is an essential requirement if you are going to get a collection started at a reasonable price. When I started collecting automata there was a flood of them on the market, due to the liquidation of King Farouk's vast (and first-rate) collection, and prices started as low as $100. This was quite a contrast to another field to which I was attracted—that of Egyptian tomb paintings. In the days of the Egyptian pharaohs it was the custom to have one's portrait painted for inclusion after death in the tomb. Many of these portraits have survived but they are eagerly sought after by museums and so have become both scarce and expensive. It just doesn't make sense to start a collection of items that cost thousands of dollars each and that are rarely offered for sale. On the other hand, thousands of Egyptian scarab seals have survived from the same period. They are attractive, individual, and interesting. They sell for a few dollars each and are freely available, so a collection can be formed both easily and inexpensively. This is far more likely to be profitable than chasing unavailable rarities, as I discovered with my automata.

A number of dealers handled them. This made it much easier to buy and sell and is a tremendously important factor in choosing a specialty, as one example will show. One of the most fascinating rarities is the automated toy of the eighteenth and nineteenth centuries. These include monkeys that perform tricks, jeweled mice that scurry about the floor, and organ grinders that play real music. The problem with these art objects is that to my knowledge there is only one dealer in the whole world specializing in them (Rita Ford in New York City) and so (except for the odd auction) purchase and sale are possible only through that one outlet, which severely restricts profit potential. Contrast this with Russian enamels made in the same period. There are dozens of dealers handling this work in every large city—the supply is adequate and as a result the price is more elastic since the dealers must compete against each other. This is definitely a better form of investment.

When I began collecting automata watches there were a dozen dealers handling them, there were monthly auctions both in New York and London, and there was a large floating supply. The reason that they have become so rare today is mostly because of a dozen collectors like myself who have gradually absorbed the dealers' stocks. Dealers usually replenish their supplies by buying up the estates of deceased collectors but the last three collectors who died left their watches to museums so the demand has continued while the supply has disappeared. Result —unbelievably high prices.

Another feature that automata offered was not so obvious, but at least as important. *There was an available supply of reference books in my chosen field.* A beginning collector knows nothing of the history, relative rarity, or even the value of pieces in his field, and while some knowledge can be picked up from dealers or at auctions, the basic nitty-gritty must be learned from books. Before entering any field check the libraries and make sure that you have at least read the basic facts. It will save you many thousands of dollars. In my field of automata watches there is one bible containing all knowledge of value in the field. It is called *Le Monde des Automata* and was published in Paris in 1928 in a limited edition of 1,000. I bought my copy in 1955 for $125, and this specialty has done so well that the book itself now sells for $1,000 and up, depending on condition!

Final point in my specialty's favor: *there are no fakes.* Because it is not possible to reproduce the intricate mechanisms of automata watches cheaply today, the field is free of forgeries. This is obviously a help to the beginner (as I mentioned on pages 26–29); when you're focusing on a specialty, try to make it a field where this kind of control is possible. Watches and clocks are always good possibilities.

Rarity, Antiquity, and Other Sacred Cows

My coups, and my failures, in the automata field have taught me that certain long-accepted guidelines for collectors are really pitfalls. One of these concerns the rarity of the object you're thinking of buying. "There are millions of those around," people will tell you. "Don't touch it—you'll never be able to get rid of it." Don't always believe them. I bought a lovely teeter-totter watch showing an angel and a butterfly balancing on a seesaw (or teeter-totter) while a seated woman plays her lyre—it was a beautiful thing but not terribly rare. It cost me $1,000 in New York in 1959, and I bought it knowing there were many other specimens of the same kind of watch to be had. Today it is worth about $5,000, and I think I'd have no problem whatsoever "getting rid of it."

As a matter of fact, extreme rarity can prove to be a hazard, so beware.

Automata wrist watches are very rare, and to my knowledge only two have been made, both by the Minerva Watch Company in Geneva in 1921. I managed to buy one, a minute repeater; the two figures hammer out the hour, quarter hour, and minute. I paid $1,500 for it in 1968, but it is hard to put a current value on it because with its rarity there is neither demand nor market. The old principle of pump-priming works in the art market as it works in other markets: unless enough people have seen or heard of the product in question, they won't know they want it. And if a demand doesn't develop, to whom can you sell?

Another myth that many collectors accept without question is that older is always better—that an antique object must be more valuable than an object of more recent vintage. My automata collection soon taught me differently. I bought two examples of a kind of pocket watch called a sector watch, in which the figure on the watch face indicates the time by pointing to the hour with one hand and the minute with the other when a button on the side of the watch is pressed. One of my purchases has a figure of Liberty on the face, and was made in 1820 in Paris. I found it in a Paris shop in 1961—the price was $1,800. My other watch has a Chinese figure on the face, and was made exactly one hundred years later. I purchased it—from an ad run last year by a New York dealer—for almost the same price as I had paid for the older one.

Another example is to compare Hobbema, an acknowledged master painter of three hundred years ago, with Renoir, his twentieth-century equivalent. A good Hobbema will sell for $35,000, while a large Renoir might bring ten times that price.

One of the most attractive, if amusing, myths about art is that erotica is a collector's item. Picasso's erotic lithographs and limited editions of pornographic books—all have been widely touted. But erotica is *not* a good investment. I purchased an erotic pocket watch—erotic figures are not uncommon in automata—which shows two figures ringing the hours, and a goat standing below them, nodding his head. But if a secret slide is pushed on the bottom of the watch the goat disappears and a couple is revealed making love. Erotic watches—myths aside—are worth far less than nonerotic automata. This one sold for $300 in 1956 and today would bring about $900.

All erotic antiques have a very limited market. Museums won't touch them and most are hardly suitable for exhibition in a private home. There is a tremendous quantity of such material available and the wise investor should keep away from it. It is just too tough to resell.

Damaged Goods

After listing all the caveats the novice collector must remember, it's nice to mention a factor you *don't* have to be wary of. Don't be afraid to buy an object because it is damaged in some way—always provided that the damage is compensated for by a reasonable price, and that you can see some way to restore or repair the piece. My favorite story—every one of us has at least one great story—concerns an apparently mortally wounded clock. This clock was made in London in 1755 and shipped to Peking the following year, where it was placed in a pavilion of the Forbidden City. There it remained until the Boxer Rebellion in 1899. Following the lifting of the siege of Peking in 1901 the clock was stolen from the palace by an English officer who took it back to England. In the 1930s it was purchased by multimillionaire Greek shipowner Sir Basil Ionides, and following his death in 1954 it and twenty other similar clocks were auctioned at Sotheby's. I bought it by mail from the picture in the catalog for $1,600—I had given a maximum bidding price of $5,000 and was pleasantly shocked to find that I had gotten it so cheaply. My pleasure evaporated when it arrived and I found there were dozens of broken and missing parts.

It took almost a year to restore the clock—a silversmith restored the facade, a jeweler replaced the stones, an artisan refugee from Egypt hand-built the trees growing from the flower pots and the lions' heads, and a brilliant one-armed clockmaker named Walter Deer put the mechanism into working order. Corning Glass spent months trying to duplicate the hollow, twisted glass rods that made an illusory "waterfall" above the clock's face; the workmen at Corning finally gave up, saying that the art had been lost over the centuries. They faked the broken rods by using spiral frosting on round glass, then gave me the rods free "because if we charged you for the man-hours we put in you couldn't afford it." The total cost of the repairs was $1,800. The clock is now worth in excess of $50,000.

Today the clock is in perfect working order and runs for seven days at a winding (Figure 14). Every hour the numerous waterfalls come to life, a series of sailing vessels pass under the face of the clock, a procession of musicians marches across the top playing their instruments, and surmounting all, a ruby pineapple slowly revolves.

This clock typifies the best in art investment. It is beautiful, it is interesting, it has given me years of pleasure, and I bought it cheaply and saw it soar in price. The additional lesson to be learned here is that huge profits can be made by purchasing and restoring damaged art objects.

These are all good general guidelines to follow when you're choosing what to invest in—I've included a more specific checklist of suggested investment programs in the ninth chapter—but the final decision about what sort of art to buy rests with you, the buyer. The most important rule to obey when you're preparing to make a purchase is the rule with which I began this chapter: buy what you like, and only what you like. That way you can never be cheated of full value.

III

WHEN

TO

BUY

This is a good time to invest in art. The last three years have seen a tremendous shakeout in almost all art fields but the trend has now turned and a larger art buying public than ever before is emerging. This is partially because of the steady growth in the teaching of art history and also because the museums are now aggressively buying. One New York art dealer (Wildenstein) boasted that in the last week of October 1976, fifty representatives of different museums visited his gallery searching for articles for their museums. Another factor is that huge funds like Artemis have now been set up in cooperation with European banks to purchase works of art in the United States for investment the same way that mutual funds buy stocks. Similarly the British Railways pension fund has allotted $10,000,000 to buy art, and a similar fund has been set up in Spain. These funds will absorb a lot of art work—and will push prices up as they do.

Timing is obviously essential in making any investment —stories of successful investors' coups invariably hinge on someone's having bought Xerox or Boise Cascade when the price was down and reselling at a profit when the stock's value had reached its peak. The same principle applies in the art world, although to the untrained analyst the highs and lows may seem a bit more difficult to detect. One very good rule to follow is *not* to buy an artist or a type of art immediately after it has received a great deal of publicity—the prices tend to be too high. That is why articles in art magazines or newspapers are not reliable as guides to investment value. A perfect example was the work of the artist Buffet, whose prices skyrocketed immediately after he was featured in the leading art magazines, and then plummeted within months. Today the darlings of the art magazines are objects of American or Canadian folk art—whose prices have soared to more than fifty times their original value in just a few years. The problem here is that these objects have been over-promoted, and the objects themselves—quilts, cooking utensils, weather vanes, crockery, large signs, and the like—have a very definite "look" that is not always compatible with a collector's other objects or his life-style. Often, too, folk art objects are large and therefore have a built-in display problem. In any case, the market has been pushed up about as far as it can be; stay away from folk art.

If you want to "buy low and sell high" in the best entrepreneurial tradition, you have to look out for real opportunities, and one of these involves other people's misery.

Revolutions

It is a sad fact that the best buys are made following a war or a revolution. The dispossessed sell their treasures for cash or food and the victors often are happy to trade their victims' treasures for foreign exchange. Thus the best buys of Chinese art ever made took place in Europe in 1901 following the looting of the summer palace, and the best and cheapest European medieval art was sold by the Russian communists in 1921. The same pattern has continued up to the present: I bought a set of fine bone china plates with gold rims that had been confiscated in Cuba in 1963 after its owner fled to Florida. Castro sold this along with thousands of other treasures to a Canadian dealer in order to get ready cash. On principle I usually avoid such purchases, but my willpower crumbled when I saw the plates carried my initials and a price tag of one dollar each. Today similar plates sell for $60 each.

Some of the greatest buys in Oriental art have been made possible by the upheavals to which China has been subject since the beginning of the century, and smart investors will always look for values in Orientalia. The 1911 revolution in China forced the abdication of the last Manchu emperor, Henry Pu Yi, although he was allowed to retain his title as emperor and was given a residence in the Forbidden City, until he was evicted by the republican government in 1924. The following year the contents of his palace were auctioned: among them was a table, made in 1850, which had sat in the Cloudless Heaven Palace. It was sold for

41

$20 to a lucky visiting Torontonian and brought to Canada, where I bought it in 1973 for $600. Sometimes you have to be alert to grasp an opportunity like this, but sometimes the opportunity simply stares you in the face.

One such encounter with chance presented itself to me last July when I was invited to lead a trade delegation on a visit to China. The Chinese government representative who was shepherding us on our trip put it to me tactfully: "When you arrive in Peking we will take you to a warehouse filled with antiques that have been donated to the government of China by formerly wealthy persons in gratitude for their liberation." Even after that introduction I was overwhelmed when I saw the warehouse, or rather the series of warehouses; one contains old ceramics, one holds old furniture, one has ancient paintings, and one is filled with miscellaneous antiques. These four warehouses in turn are fed from a mass of other buildings filled with the effects of the "formerly wealthy" Chinese. (I asked point-blank if this material had been confiscated and was blandly assured that that was not the case—it had all been purchased "from the people"; it is true that in every city in China there is a shop in the downtown district whose function is to purchase antiques and old jewelry.) These items are of absolutely no value in present-day China—no woman wears jewelry, and living quarters are so cramped that there is little space to display antiques—so the prices on all this material are staggeringly low. I purchased a dozen paintings on silk, each measuring 8 feet by 3 feet and showing a family scene in a landscape in bright unfaded colors, for $100 apiece; each was accompanied by a government certificate guaranteeing that it was at least 125 years old. I later found that similar paintings sold in Hong Kong for $300 and in Toronto for $600.

In the same series of warehouses, jade necklaces dating back to 1800 were offered at prices ranging from $150 up to $300. Enameled spoons, forks, and knives sold for $10 each while 125-year-old beautifully decorated opium pipes were priced from $20 to $60. The same kind of pipe was being offered in the antique shops in Peking for $100 and up, and modern copies were being sold in Hong Kong for about $150. Ceramics dating back to the Ming period filled one entire warehouse, and for $800 I purchased a perfect, translucent, paper-thin bowl dated 1805. When I returned to Toronto the director of the Far East Gallery of the Royal Ontario Museum was shocked that the Chinese were selling items of such quality and wistfully asked if the museum could acquire my purchase.

Because it has a history of political and social turmoil—and because it was already the site of so many fine works of art—China is possibly the world's last great art frontier. It is perhaps the only place in the world where art items can still be purchased at anywhere from one-third to one-half of the world price and where—more important even than price—the quality of some of the items will be outstanding. One of the persons in my party was hesitant about purchasing items that might have been confiscated, but after one hour in that warehouse he was buying with as much abandon as the rest of us. As he put it: "I think I have principles, but nobody has that much principle."

Obviously few people can make a trip to China even

now, but it is worth remembering that items from the warehouses may show up for resale somewhere outside of China, and they may still be underpriced in relation to their value.

Dispersals

Another great chance to buy cheaply is at the time of the dispersal of the belongings of the rich and famous. The reason is that the sale often includes so many of one kind of object that the market temporarily becomes flooded. (This happens only if a huge collection is dispersed suddenly in a field with a limited supply and demand— where there are relatively few collectors and dealers.) After about a year the dealers will have sold the large stock they have bought at the sale and prices will begin to soar: demand, stimulated by the sudden availability of a certain kind of object, will far exceed supply, and competition for remaining objects will be fierce. The sale of the treasures belonging to the Egyptian King Farouk was a classic example of such an opportunity. Farouk had amassed a very high quality collection of exquisitely beautiful watches with moving figures on the face and musical mechanisms within, which had been produced in the last quarter of the eighteenth century by the collaboration of watchmakers, jewelers, dealers in precious stones, setters, engravers, enamelers, and enamel painters. After the Egyptian revolution in 1953 his collection was sold at auction in Cairo and I was able to buy a few lovely pieces from the catalog. One is a watch with a tiny mill scene on the face: the waterwheel turns and water flows down from it while the fisherman periodically raises his line to see if he has caught anything and the two workers below saw on the log. I got it for $1,000 and it would bring about $18,000 today.

Also from the Farouk sale I got a snuffbox with a watch on its enameled top. The top opens to reveal two articulated figures who play a tune every hour: while the lady strums her instrument, the gentleman counts the beat (Figure 15). I find it most incredible that the Egyptian government sold it to me for only $150 in 1954 (Figure 16). Today it would bring about $10,000.

Grasping the Nettle

There are some moments—absolutely unpredictable and uncategorizable—when you must seize the opportunity to buy no matter what the risks are. A sort of sixth sense will tell you: buy this, and buy it now. Obey it. Each of us in our lifetimes will have a few chances to make a real killing, but usually we won't take the chance because we are afraid of the risks. Remember, *no one gets rich without taking risks.* When an opportunity presents itself, make the most of it. I call this process grasping the nettle.

I've missed some of my opportunities and like everyone else I regret them immensely—I will never forget turning down an exquisite and huge Pissarro in Paris in 1956. (I thought the price of $10,000 was excessive! Today it is worth at least $250,000.) But I have never regretted taking a chance or making a purchase regardless of how it turned out. Those that turn out well are so sweet that they far overshadow all the others.

Of course the first step in grasping the nettle is learning how to recognize an opportunity when it presents itself. This in itself is not difficult. One prime example occurred in 1972 at a show of the finest Chinese crafts put on in Canada by the People's Republic. Among the items in the show was an unusually large turquoise carving (Figure 17). I was terribly impressed by the exhibition and asked the representative of the Chinese government if I could buy one of the hardstone or ivory pieces. He explained that the Chinese had in fact decided to sell the collection but that Neiman-Marcus had contracted to buy the entire lot. He added with a broad smile, "It's the best deal I ever had. The Chinese wanted seventy thousand dollars for the collection and Neiman-Marcus has offered me two hundred and fifty thousand. If you want to buy one piece why don't you contact their representative?"

I put the entire thing out of my mind, but one week later, just one day before the exhibition was to close, I received a frantic phone call. It was the businessman representative, who told me, "The Neiman-Marcus buyer arrived in Toronto this morning and collapsed with a heart attack at the airport. He is unable to close the deal and I must come up with the money within twenty-four hours." He offered to sell me the lot of 196 pieces for $125,000. I didn't have that kind of money but offered him $70,000, which brought forth an indignant refusal.

One hour later he called back to accept the $70,000. I didn't have 70,000 cents available, but I managed to borrow the money that afternoon from a wealthy business acquaintance. There were about eighty pieces of the same quality as the turquoise carving in the collection—and the turquoise piece is worth about $18,000 today.

It is almost impossible to plan for a "nettle-grasping" situation, because it will crop up unexpectedly—sometimes just because you are in the right place at the right time. One of the most spectacular examples of how this principle works is the story of a businessman who happened to be in Hong Kong during the summer of 1950 and happened to buy a magnificent coral carving for the unremarkable price of $300. It turned out that the piece had been part of the Sassoon family's collection of Chinese art in Shanghai and that the Chinese government had sold it, after the family's precipitous flight from China in 1948, to raise foreign exchange. The piece has an estimated worth of between $35,000 and $45,000 today.

There is no way that businessman could have known for a certainty that the coral piece would be worth as much as it was; but there is a kind of instinctual knowledge that comes to you in a situation like this. Learn to listen to the voice inside you that says, "This is something good." Obey it, even when your "rational" self tells you you're crazy. In 1961 I was window-shopping in Cannes and happened to glance into an antique shop that was displaying a large and beautiful piece in rose quartz. The carving was 300 years old and the price tag on it was a steep $6,000. Somehow I knew I should buy it, although all my reasoning told me I was overpaying and would regret it. My reasoning, it turns out, was wrong, and my instincts were right: the piece is worth $25,000 today.

Not all the risks you take need be quite so heavy—there are some nettles you can grasp that will cost you less than $500. Just recently, in 1974, my wife found an exquisite silk shawl (Figure 18) in a Madrid antique shop, where she paid $400 for it. The so-called Spanish shawl actually originated in China and was exported to Spain and Portugal; this was one of many produced by female slave labor in Shanghai in 1921 and then shipped to the Philippines where they had a brief vogue. Beautiful examples can still be found in Spain from anywhere from $300 to $500.

Perhaps the most important rule governing when to buy is this: never be afraid to sail against the wind. Ignore fashion and buy for aesthetic reasons and inevitably, if you are patient, you will see your judgment justified. Fashion in art comes and goes depending on the fluctuations of "new money"—sixty years ago huge English portraits were the rage at prices between $50,000 and $200,000, but today the fashion has altered and those pictures cannot be sold at any price. At the same time that English paintings were so sought after, no one wanted to buy beautiful hand-painted eighteenth-century snuffboxes, available for less than $100. Today these boxes are eagerly sought after at $10,000 and up.

The examples I've mentioned above are just more reminders of a point stressed throughout this book: you should stay away from over-promoted art and art objects.

Paintings, furnishings, and objects executed in the so-called "Style Moderne," or Art Deco, are all the rage now, and Art Deco lamps, vases, cigarette boxes, statuettes, chairs, mirrors, or tables command vastly inflated prices. Now is not the time to buy into this field—if indeed it ever is. These objects are for those with very special tastes and will not appeal to everyone, so beware of them. The same is true of American Western art, which is overvalued right now, Tiffany glass, modern graphics by acknowledged masters, and blue-and-white china—to name just a few high-priced items. All of these have been seen in glossy magazines or sold in well-publicized sales, and their prices are consequently at an all-time high. So don't buy them. Have the courage to go against fashion, and look for the values that fashion has passed over.

Later in the book (see pages 111–126) I'll list some of today's neglected beauties; for now, I'll just repeat my advice. Sail against the wind.

IV

WHERE
TO
BUY

Once you've decided what to buy and have considered whether now is the time to buy it, you are armed for battle. But where do you begin? I've known many people —beginning art investors—who are truly at a loss at this point, for the art market is by and large a closed little world, and newcomers simply do not know their way in it. But they must learn, and learn fast, because where you make your purchase has a profound and direct effect on the price you will pay for it, and hence on the profit you can ultimately expect to make.

There are three matters to consider under this heading —the locale of one's purchase, the merits of auction houses, and the cost of buying from a dealer.

Buy at the Source

It is always cheapest to buy art where it is produced, and it makes excellent sense to be on the lookout for local folk art when you are traveling—whether it's for business or pleasure. The difference in the price paid for an object at its source and the same object in a New York shop can be horrendous, and the reason is obvious: the U.S. dealer must pay almost the same local price as the tourist and then he must add in insurance, transportation, duty, the cost of sales help, rent, and his profit.

The black "pearls" of Cozumel are a perfect example. These are not pearls at all but a form of coral that grows in the Mexican waters off Cozumel Island. I purchased a perfect strand in Mexico in 1975 for $85, while its duplicate sold at that time on Fifth Avenue for $300. Today similar pearls bring at least $500 in New York. Not a bad appreciation for an investment!

There are fine opportunities for the collector and the investor in the folk painting of the Caribbean islands, notably Haiti. On a trip there in 1968 I found a painting, a village scene, by the artist Casimir, who has become famous for his portrayals of colorful island life. He sold the painting to me for $50. *The New York Times* featured Casimir's work three years ago, and since then the price of his paintings has soared to $3,000 and up, but similar paintings by equally good artists can still be bought in Port-au-Prince for about $100.

Of course there is no guarantee that *The New York Times* will run a story on any of these other artists—that was just blind luck—but the risk is so small and the possible profit so great that if you do go to Haiti you should add $100 to the cost of your trip and bring home a painting. You may end up recouping the entire expense.

Haiti is of course not the only place to buy contempo-

rary folk art. The trick in picking a potentially good investment is to seek out handmade articles, indigenous to the
area. The vicuna rugs of Bolivia, the shawls of Ecuador,
and the pottery of Japan fall into this category. So-called
folk art that is mass-produced, on the other hand—like
Canadian Eskimo carvings, Irish linen, Hong Kong ivory,
or most African art—does not.

It pays to keep a sharp eye out when traveling. In 1975
my wife and I visited Jordan and I drove down through
the desert to the red city of Petra. At a water stop a veiled
Bedouin woman came by with her husband, children,
goats, and camels—a magnificent sight, but what caught
my eye was her striking silver necklace (Figure 19). After
fifteen minutes of bargaining I traded her husband $25 for
the necklace, and he offered to throw the lady into the
deal for another $15. The coins in the necklace turned out
to be Roman from the second century.

I had no expertise in either old jewelry or old coins but
I was attracted by the beauty of the necklace and the fact
that such things are just not sold in my part of the world.
If you are off the beaten path it is foolish not to gamble a
few dollars for things that are handmade, unusual, and un-
available at home.

Even if you're not off the beaten path but simply close
to the source, you can find amazing bargains in art objects
that can be immediately resold for a profit should you wish
to do so. If you are traveling to Hong Kong, or know
someone who will be, try to pick up some of the inlaid
metalwork being done in China today. For the most part
· it is hammered silver, dipped in gold, and then inlaid

with semiprecious stones. I bought two humidors worked in this manner; they are surprisingly cheap considering the work involved and the value of the material, and they were an excellent investment. They cost $250 each in Hong Kong and can be resold for about $600 each in New York.

Sometimes amazing bargains are picked up simply because you are in a place where no one else goes. In 1958 I visited Shanghai and found that there were absolutely no tourists because of the U.S. embargo. In a large department store I found a beautiful small carving for sale at $8 at the jade counter. Today it is worth about $500. (I try not to think of the larger pieces which were offered then—with no takers—for about $100 each.)

On the same trip I also was able to find some marvelous semi-antique ivory pieces: a hanging basket with a Chinese village carved in the base and dozens of little roses in the top for $80, which would cost about $800 in a Hong Kong antique store, an entire ivory tusk carved to represent the Empress Dowager's summer palace (Figure 20) for $150, which could bring over $1,000 at auction in the United States today, and a complicated ivory carving representing an entire village for $100, which would fetch ten times its price on the current market.

One of the reasons I could get such a bargain price was that, due to the U.S. embargo, no American could bring home such jade or ivory pieces. This principle works to the benefit of American tourists in some places where foreigners get opportunities that local buyers do not: every communist country has shops which their own nationals may not enter and which sell antiques for hard currency to foreigners only.

It is not always so easy to buy art works for export, however. In Mongolia all ancient art has been declared the property of the state: most of the monasteries (formerly storehouses of art treasures) have been closed and the few that remain open are under strict communist control. No art objects are allowed to leave the country, and departing travelers are usually closely searched. I visited Mongolia in 1966 and I doubt if there is a harder and hardier country in the world—certainly there can be no more rapacious bureaucrats anywhere. On my last night in Ulan Bator a frightened former monk came to my hotel room and traded me two ancient figures of gods (Figure 21) in return for $50 in U.S. greenbacks. Neither of us understood the other's language and I have no idea what use he had for the U.S. money, but I am very happy with my purchase, although I was petrified with fear as I boarded the plane with them in my side pocket.

Normally I strictly obey the export regulations of the country I am visiting, but the Mongolian government officials were so hostile and unkind that I was happy to have the opportunity to break one of their laws. My profit in this case, incidentally, was largely emotional and aesthetic, since Mongolian art is so rare in the West that there is very little demand for it on the open market. Not that I want to sell my figurines—I had too good an adventure acquiring them. But if I change my mind I can always "make something" on them by giving them to a museum for a tax credit (see pages 94–100).

Art comes in many forms, and frequently an object that is utilitarian—or at the most decorative—in its place of origin is a real, and valuable, work of art. One example is the sari—the Indian woman's garment. In the holy city of Benares on the Ganges River, women and children labor with gold thread to make beautiful ornamental saris and stoles. I saw a lovely piece produced on a 1959 visit and paid $65 for it. The same stole sold then in New York for $400, and today the New York price would be over $1,000. Bear in mind when making such purchases that it is the heavily worked, elaborate pieces that tend to go way up in price. It is unwise to purchase plain saris or stoles for investment purposes, no matter how inexpensive they are.

Another ornamental "utility" item that you can get at its source is the North African rug, especially the thick quilted carpets made in Morocco by children. I bought one in December 1975, and it cost me $50. The children are paid $1 for a nine-hour day—they work six days a week.

When I expressed dismay to my guide that six-year-olds should be working like this he replied, "Better work than starve—we are poor in this country." Leaving aside the moral question, these rugs are the cheapest in the world, and the same rug that sells for $50 in Azrou will sell for $100 in Casablanca and $300 in New York or Toronto. If you don't mind walking on the fruits of child labor these rugs are a good investment even at New York prices.

One popular item that is probably *not* a good buy, even at the source, is the antique Oriental rug. Old rugs have been one of the best investments of the 1970s, and the price of an average old Persian or Afghan rug has multiplied ten times in the last four years as a huge wave of buying has engulfed those rugs put up for sale. But these rugs are too much in demand: because of this huge price surge, I most definitely do not recommend their purchase —in fact I think this is the right time to sell out and cash in.

If you are interested in fine ornamental glasswork, you should know that Czech glass blowers are still turning out the finest and most beautiful glass in the world. I bought some current—not antique—examples in Prague in 1970: stemmed wineglasses in colored and etched glass. The Czechs sell them for $20 each. Their price is bound to soar—in North America they already retail around $50 and will go up from there—because the cost of labor even in Czechoslovakia is soaring and few young workers today are willing to subject themselves to the many years of impoverished apprenticeship.

Bear in mind, however, that this glass is fragile; its fragility carries with it the danger of breakage.

The Local Corollary

The corollary to the rule about buying at the source is that you can buy an object more cheaply *away* from the place in which it has local associations. When you travel, search antique shops for items that you know to have local value at home; the dealer from whom you buy them will not have any idea of the associations they may have, and you can usually pick up such things very cheaply. This is what happened to me when I found Sir Henry Pellatt's tea service.

Sir Henry Pellatt was an eccentric millionaire who built an incredible dream castle in Toronto in 1911 at a cost of three million dollars. He stuffed it with art treasures and when he went broke these were all dispersed. Among the items sold was his tea service, which was auctioned off for $40 in Depression year 1933. I bought it for $240 in 1953. Because it was Pellatt's it would bring at least $2,000 in Toronto today.

The name of Henry Pellatt means nothing in the United States, and so I was able to buy Pellatt's silver wine taster for $3 at a Miami antique fair in 1976. Back home in Toronto that same wine taster is worth $250. If you are traveling, it's always worth browsing through flea markets or antique shops, looking for items from your hometown. They can be worth much, much more when you get them back home. Incidentally, no matter where you make your purchase, it is wise to avoid consummating it in New York City because of its punitive sales tax. Clever investors who are making expensive purchases should use an address— either their own, or that of a friend—out-of-state: this can save hundreds or even thousands of dollars.

Dealers vs. Auctions

Of course it isn't always possible to buy art objects at their source: not everyone travels as frequently or as far as I do, for example, and there are art objects (Impressionist paintings, fine eighteenth-century furniture, or Renaissance manuscripts, among other things) that have no clearly definable locale.

This is where the buyer must go either to a dealer who specializes in the kind of work the buyer wants, or to an auction, where the goods are being sold to the highest bidder. Which is the best way?

The beginning collector is usually better off to start by buying from a dealer rather than an auction house because he can lean on that dealer for advice until he becomes experienced in the field. This is how I began and I have never regretted it. Buying at auction you are on your own and if you overpay it's just too bad, but with a reputable dealer you can take the object home on approval. If you do decide to buy, most dealers will allow you to return it within one year for a full credit (i.e., you can change it for something else—most don't give back cash).

Another advantage to working with a good dealer is that he will keep his eyes open for pieces that will be of interest to you and if you are a good customer will give you first crack at them. Remember also that dealers give each other a 20-percent discount. Try to get friendly with one dealer in your hometown—if you give him some business he may be willing to allow you to use his name to make the odd purchase elsewhere at a 20-percent discount.

In selecting a dealer in the United States, a good earmark of reliability is the dealer's membership in the Art Dealers' Association of America. The A.D.A. is an organization devoted to improving the standards of art dealing, keeping fakes off the market, and ensuring a fair shake for the collecting public; its members have all demonstrated complete professionalism in their dealings, as well as a comprehensive knowledge of a specific field of art, an ability to spot a fake, and a history of having made some contribution to the cultural life of the community. Membership in this organization is by invitation only, and of the many thousands of dealers in the United States only ninety-seven have met the A.D.A.'s rigid requirements; so if you fix on a dealer with an A.D.A. designation, you're in good hands.

Once you know your way in the art market, you will probably do very much better buying at auction than you will buying the same or a similar object from a dealer, for it is at the auction houses that dealers make many of their own purchases. Be careful, though: buying at auction carries many dangers—most serious of which is that of buying a fake. There are literally dozens of small auction houses in the United States and Canada that will sell whatever is offered to them. If you know your subject and can tell the good from the bad—in other words, if you have specialized in a field—real bargains can be picked up in country auctions or at flea markets. Often the auctioneer doesn't know what he is selling; I'll never forget my experience in Pittsburgh, where I wandered into a storefront auctioneer's and purchased a seventeenth-century crystal watch for $120. This kind of thing does happen occasionally, but you must know your field—because dealers will often use an auctioneer or market of this kind as an outlet for damaged or fake goods. The same caveat applies to the country auctioneer—and there is unfortunately no way to tell the honest ones from the crooks.

If you are serious about investing, there are some outstanding auction houses that will stand behind everything they sell—Parke Bernet in New York and Sotheby's, Phillip's and Christie's in London.

Another hazard of purchasing at auction is that of being carried away by the excitement and the competition. To avoid this, set a firm top price in your mind before the auction begins and *never* let yourself go above that figure. If you are careful about fakes and about bidding, you should do very well at auction houses.

Buying from dealers for investment purposes is very tricky. It is hard to make money on such an investment because the dealer's markup will range from 40 to 100 percent and the value of the art object must move up that huge amount before you can begin to profit, so as a general rule I tend to avoid such purchases. On the other hand the good dealers will stand behind their sales, will guarantee the authenticity of their material, and will buy the item back if requested. Also it should be noted that the good dealers have the very finest items for sale, and if you wish to flesh out a collection with a specific piece, that may be the only route to follow. I have had very happy experiences with the fine dealers I have worked with and have made money on almost all of my purchases from them. These include Wartski's in London, Edgar Mannheimer in Zurich, Paul Schaeffer in New York, and Blair

Laing and Simon Dresdnere in Toronto. Sometimes it's worth paying more in order to get the best.

The only intelligent way to choose a dealer is by his reputation. The location of his shop, the amount of advertising he does, the size of his stock are all unimportant in comparison with how he treats his clients. Before beginning to trade with any dealer I always inquire about him at the local public art gallery or museum. If he receives praise all is well, but if the curator is noncommittal —beware!

A group of doctor friends of mine ignored this rule to their peril and purchased a collection of Southeast Asian art from a prominent Toronto dealer in Orientalia. They paid him $80,000 on the basis of their many years of friendship, with the intention of donating the collection to a public museum. The museum took one look and shipped it all back to them, saying much of it was fake and it was all overvalued. The dealer refused to take back the collection.

V

HOW

TO

BUY

Having decided what you want to invest in and where you will go to find it, how do you actually begin to buy? The first thing *not* to do is to walk into a gallery or auction house and buy the first attractive piece in view. Before buying anything a successful collector should learn the basic rules or he may very well begin collecting by buying something that cannot be resold at any price. And the first rule is to avoid fakery.

If you're going to buy at auction—if, for example, an auction house is selling a large consignment of goods from an estate sale and you know the late owner had some pieces you are interested in—the first thing you should do is get a catalog for the sale. The auctioneers will usually send one on request. The catalog will provide you with the kind of information you might ordinarily get by asking a dealer, such as an artist's name and dates, the size, date, and medium of the work, and so on. Once you have found something you like, use your catalog, or your questions to the dealer, to find out more about it. Learn an object's history. There is a dual importance to this because history affects value even if the object is not a fake.

Determining Provenance

The pedigree of an art object is important first because it helps to authenticate the object and give it a history. Every few years a newspaper article appears describing the discovery of a previously unknown Rembrandt found by a sharp-eyed collector in an attic or covered by dust in the rear of a junk shop. It is almost a certainty that these paintings are not real Rembrandts, for everything Rembrandt did was cataloged long ago; these new finds are either fraudulent or self-delusionary. What distinguishes the real Rembrandts is their provenance—the list of verifiable former owners and places of exhibition. One basic rule in art purchasing is never to make an expensive purchase when the dealer is reluctant or unable to reveal the provenance. Chances are the object is either fake or stolen.

Knowing an object's provenance also enables you to identify its previous owners—which will enhance the object's value if it was owned by a famous person—as were the watches purchased from the Farouk sale. But while you can ask a dealer to supply documentation of an object's provenance, you cannot do this with auction houses. There, you take what you get. However, a careful study of the catalog may help you here. The London houses use a simple code to describe each painting. If the artist's name is given in full, e.g., Cornelius Krieghoff, it means that the house guarantees the painting's authenticity. If the painting is listed as being by C. Krieghoff, the auctioneer is unsure and will not give a guarantee. If the painting is listed as by Krieghoff, it is a fake done in the manner of Krieghoff. Parke Bernet uses a similar system for art objects made in the last one hundred years, but for items created before then they give only their best opinion in descending order of merit, e.g., "Cornelius Krieghoff," "attributed to Cornelius Krieghoff," "circle of Cornelius Krieghoff," "school of Cornelius Krieghoff," "manner of Cornelius Krieghoff," down to the lowly "after Cornelius Krieghoff," which means that the painting is a copy of Krieghoff's style by some unknown painter.

When There Is No Provenance

Despite all the means available to check provenance, it sometimes becomes impossible to trace, and forgeries continue to find their way into all types of collections.

Purchasers of fakes range from the rankest beginner (such as I was when I bought my "Gainsborough") to the wealthiest and most sophisticated collector. Thus in 1962 Ottawa's National Gallery borrowed 187 paintings by Matisse, Picasso, and Degas from Walter P. Chrysler, the auto millionaire. After the collection went on exhibit, sixty of the paintings proved to be fakes. And in 1967, New

York's Metropolitan Museum of Art admitted with some embarrassment that its famous 2,400-year-old bronze horse, purchased by the Met in 1923, was a fake made only fifty years earlier.

The Met was not the first institution to be embarrassed. There was a great scandal in Rome in the second century when the Senate discovered that ancient Greek pots being sold in that city were modern fakes!

And don't pay too much attention to that official-looking certificate signed by an expert guaranteeing a painting's authenticity. In his diary Paris dealer René Gimpel* wrote back in 1929:

"The Berlin dealers," Armand told me, "engaged the prettiest typists in town to send to B., who was senile, to ask for certificates of authentication." Armand saw the indisputable expert write scandalous testimonials and was amazed to hear him say: "But I couldn't refuse, she had such pretty legs."

The same comedy continues these days with his successor, Friedlander, who is madly in love with a dealer's wife. If she slept with him it would be quickly finished, so she keeps her garters fastened. On the basis of such certificates, American collections are formed!

If I had been aware of the prevalence of worthless authentication certificates, I might have avoided the purchase of my "antique" Judaica pointer, described on page 26. In that case my certificate of authenticity from the dealer (Figure 22) turned out to be worthless.

With the vast number of fakes in circulation the non-

* *Diary of an Art Dealer* (New York: Farrar, Straus & Giroux, 1969).

65

expert buyer often doesn't know where to turn to have a prospective purchase checked for authenticity. The one place that has no ax to grind and that can actually give a quick, accurate answer is your own museum. In my city the Royal Ontario Museum has a regular Wednesday afternoon clinic to which individuals may bring objects for authenticating. (One thing you should not expect from your museum is a valuation.)

If your museum cannot give you an authentication quickly, and if you don't mind paying for this service, the International Foundation for Art Research at 654 Madison Avenue, New York City, will examine a painting and will give a written report as to its authorship. The foundation is completely reliable, for they have available not only expert examiners but also the most modern scientific tools, but they are not cheap—expect a minimum cost of $300.

The rule for the potential buyer is—Beware! My rule of thumb is very simple. I buy only beautiful objects and pay for them only what they are worth to me as a beautiful object—and I always proceed as if everything is brand-new. In any case where the name of the maker or the age of the object enhances the value, I insist on knowing the provenance, and I have learned the hard way never to buy such objects at a bargain price from a private person or small gallery.

Typical was the dealer who came to Toronto last June from San Francisco with an impressive collection of paintings by Goya, Rembrandt, and Vermeer. He explained to prospective buyers that this was a private sale forced on the owner by financial difficulties and for that reason no names could be given. When I was called in for my opinion I asked that I be given the owner's name in confidence and when this was refused I offered to return the next day with an expert in fakes and stolen goods currently working with our police department. When we returned at the appointed hour, the dealer had checked out, leaving no forwarding address. On the other hand, legitimate galleries are very careful to preserve their reputation and great shops will always both stand behind their objects and be happy to tell their history.

Finances

Once you are satisfied that your would-be purchase is an original, the next step is to decide how much you are prepared to pay for it. At a reputable dealer's the price will be marked and will usually be firm, although on large purchases it is quite in order to ask for a 10-percent reduction. At an auction house it is just as easy—the "big three" auctioneers supply their estimate of an item's value to all prospective bidders in advance of a sale, and they are usually quite accurate. You should, however, be prepared to pay 10 to 20 percent more than the estimated price.

And how do you pay for it? Today it may no longer be necessary to have all the money in hand before making an art purchase, for American banks are now beginning to finance such purchases. This is a relatively new development; traditionally banks have shied away from this type of loan because of the difficulties in valuation of prospective purchases, the relative illiquidity involved in the investment, the lack of potential income, the problems of storage and authenticity, and—most of all—the banker's almost total lack of knowledge of the art market. The banker's attitude could be summed up in the story told by George Le Maistre, a director of the Federal Deposit Insurance Corporation, about the antique-car collector who discovered a 1950 Rolls in perfect condition and approached his banker for financing. He was turned down with a bland, "Sorry—we don't finance used cars!"

Happily, this attitude began to change five years ago when the Commonwealth National Bank in Dallas began to finance art purchases. That bank has now made four hundred loans ranging from $250 up to $400,000, with an average loan of $5,000; it has not suffered a single loss. The loans are all arranged with repayment on an installment basis at an interest rate of 11½ percent over a period of up to five years. The success of Commonwealth encouraged other bankers, and now Manufacturers Hanover and Finance America Credit Corporation (a subsidiary of the Bank of America) in New York City and the Amalgamated Trust and Savings Bank in Chicago are willing to make loans on art purchases giving up to 50 percent of the market or appraised value.

If you are seeking such a loan, either to purchase a new art piece or to raise money against something you already own, you should expect to produce evidence of ownership, proof of current value (preferably by comparison with some recent public sale), and some indication of your ability to repay the loan. The bank doesn't want to foreclose on your art object, but it does want to be repaid.

Incidentally, if you are a professional you can buy your art with the government's money by letting the art double as office decoration while it increases in value. Perfectly legitimate and entirely deductible.

A rush of this type of buying by doctors and lawyers in the southwestern United States has resulted in a tremendous boom in Western American art with prices multiplying enormously in just a few years: Harry Jackson issued forty copies of his "Pony Express" ten years ago at $3,000 each and they now sell for over $20,000.

Making Your Purchase

When you've determined how much you're willing to give for the object of your choice, make your offer. It is not necessary, when buying at auction, to be there in person; most reputable auction firms will be glad to accept a bid by mail or telephone. Send in your top bid and the auctioneer will consider it as official as if you had made it from the floor—you won't end up offering considerably more than anyone else bid, because the auctioneer will bid for you as though you were there and will not start with your top price. And you will have avoided the risk of getting carried away by the bidding. Proxy bids are most useful in buying art objects that are sold abroad; you can buy the goods without having to make the trip for them. The auction house will see that they are shipped to you according to your instructions (you must obviously pay shipping and handling), and the best part of it all is that you won't have to pay customs duty on your purchase when you import it—all antiques and original works of art are admitted free through customs.

If you are attending the auction in person, be careful of the "Ring." This is a group of dealers who get together before every major auction and pool their bids to avoid bidding against each other and forcing their costs any higher than necessary. After the auction the Ring hold a second private auction among themselves to decide who gets each of the items they have bought, and they then split the extra funds equally among each dealer—this way the unsuccessful dealer gets a cash compensation.

The Ring, however, is not set up just to keep costs low— its members also will do everything possible to discourage non-dealers and potential customers from buying successfully at auction. I have seen them deliberately bid a piece of Fabergé far above its real value after one of them had glimpsed a wealthy collector's catalog in which he had jotted the maximum price he was prepared to pay. The Fabergé was worth $3,000 and the Ring had intended to bid a maximum of $1,800, but they pushed the bids up to $4,700, knowing that the collector was prepared to go to $5,000. They made a double gain in this way: the collector learned that it is often cheaper to buy a piece in a shop than to compete with that dealer at auction; and they set a new price level for that type of Fabergé, which increased the value of all the pieces they already owned.

Under no circumstances should you allow yourself to be rushed when making a purchase. If the dealer tells you that someone else is interested or is coming to see the piece "tomorrow," he is putting pressure on you to make a fast decision, and this should make you suspicious. A reputable dealer will never attempt to play customers off against each other, and if you are interested in a piece he should be willing to hold it for you for a few days at no charge— if he won't, you are buying from the wrong dealer.

My most recent purchase illustrates the way everyone should buy. Last summer I was on holiday in Tokyo and spotted a coffee set of painted pottery in the Imperial Hotel arcade. The price was $75, but I didn't have a clue as to what sets like that were worth or what prices were being charged by competitive shops. I asked the store-keeper to put the pottery aside for me while I comparison-shopped, and she agreed to do so. After I had visited several other shops and discovered that the original price was reasonable, I returned and completed the purchase. Similarly, buyers should not be stampeded at auctions. Prior to every auction there are several days during which the goods can be examined, and if you are in doubt about the quality of an item you are well advised to pay a specialist in the field a few dollars for his opinion. That fee will pay itself off manyfold. There is nothing worse in investing in art than overpaying. Not only are you stuck with a bad investment, but all pleasure in that object immediately disappears.

Last year I bought a heavily decorated pair of silver cigarette cases from a Toronto shop for $1,200 and just a few weeks later saw an identical pair in Hong Kong offered at $540. Not only did I feel aggrieved at the dealer and angry at myself, but I found that every time I looked at those lovely cases I felt foolish and upset. Finally, in order to get rid of my down feelings I sold the cases at a loss. It was my own fault entirely because I had ignored my rules about comparison-shopping and checking elsewhere before making any major purchase. I had just been too carried away by the cases' novel appearance.

In any purchase you can seek advice, but ultimately you must base your decision on your own judgment. I've learned the hard way that you can't leave this key matter up to anyone else—no matter how expert.

Expert and Inexpert Opinions

It is sensible and proper to go to an art expert to have an expensive piece authenticated before purchase, but as far as I am concerned authentication is the expert's only function. I most definitely do not recommend asking any of the specialists their opinion about your art investments. They seem to make the same number of mistakes as anybody else—and this rule applies even more stringently to "financial experts," bankers and brokers.

In 1965 one of Canada's largest banks hired world-famous architect Ludwig Mies van der Rohe to design for them a new Toronto headquarters. Mies van der Rohe designed a complex of towers and then, as an artist, went one step further, recommending that a collection of valuable paintings and sculptures be purchased for the bank's top-floor executive area. Mies van der Rohe felt that a few works of the highest quality could form the nucleus of a small permanent collection of international repute, and to start things off he recommended that the bank purchase pieces by Klee, Kandinsky, Cézanne, Picasso, Braque, Gris, Mondrian, Schwitters, Munch, and Matisse. They would be expensive, of course, but certainly one of the safest investments the bank could make.

Mies van der Rohe followed up his recommendations by sending the bank a list of twelve paintings that were then available for purchase at a total cost of $1,750,000. The bank officials consulted with their experts and decided to turn down Mies van der Rohe's suggestion. Instead they decorated the executive area with modern Canadian art, telling the architect: "This bank is not in the business of trying to make money from art." The bankers were more correct than they knew. Ten years later the recommended twelve paintings could have been sold for over $5½ million.

It is not just bankers and painting experts who make classic mistakes, so remember to take any opinion offered you with a grain of salt. In August 1973, New York's largest dealer in automata watches was offered a pair of Moses watches—eighteenth-century silver-dollar-sized pocket watches on which the figure of Moses strikes a rock which parts and from which water appears to flow for the thirsty Israelites who fill their cups—for $40,000. As the dealer put it to me, "Of course I did not buy them. We may have inflation but it will be many a year before our inflation is that bad." Just three months later only one of those watches went up for sale at auction at Sotheby's—the competition was fierce and the buyer paid $52,000.

Value is a matter of judgment. Don't always assume that the expert is right, but trust your own feelings, within reason. You may have less experience than a dealer or appraiser, but you also carry less of his burden of inhibitions—inhibitions caused by his knowledge of past prices. It is often easier for the amateurs to adjust to the new price levels than the expert who has had thirty years of experience.

And prices have changed quickly. In 1959 the French magazine *Plaisirs de France* calculated that $1,000 invested in the work of various artists twenty-five years earlier would have done better than investment in any stock: $1,000 in Chagall would have grown to $30,000; $1,000 in Soutine to $50,000; $1,000 in Picasso to $150,000; $1,000 in Rouault to $300,000, and $1,000 in Dufy to $600,000. Yet who could have dreamed when the magazine published their article that the following fifteen years would cause those prices to rise so much higher that they would make the boom of the previous years look like a stable period.

And this leads us to the key question. Can anyone tell when the top of this market is near—when an investor should get out?

[1]

[2]

[3]

[4]

[5]

[6]

[7]

[8]

[9]

[10]

11]

[12]

[14]

[13]

[15]

Banque Mosseri

SOCIETE ANONYME EGYPTIENNE

ADRESSE TELEGRAPHIQUE 'MOSSERIBANK'
CODES
A.B.C. 5TH EDITION
LIEBERS
BENTLEYS-PETERSON

Le Caire, le ⎯⎯⎯⎯⎯⎯⎯⎯⎯⎯

B. P. NO. 988

EN/SW

Dr. Morton Shulman

378 Roncesvalles Av.
Toronto
Canada.

Dear Sir,   PALACE COLLECTIONS OF EGYPT

   We confirm our cable of the 16th inst reading as follows;

"BOUGHT LOT 542 FOR 50 POUNDS CABLE FURTHER DIRECTIONS"

   We have insured the lot purchased for your account through

Messrs. Thos Cook & Son Ltd.', against all risks including breakage.

However, Messrs. Cook's estimated note of charge does not include

freight charges which will be debited forward.

   We will ask you to remit to us fifty ~~annexix~~ pounds, Egyptian,

plus insurance, freight, packing, and commission- the whole to be

covered by one hundred and fifty american dollars.

   Awaiting to hear from you we remain, dear Sir,

                              Yours faithfully

[16]

[17]

[18]

[19]

[20]

[21]

GALERIAS DE ANTIGÜEDADES

ABELARDO LINARES, S. A.

DIRECTORES:
ARTURO LINARES
ANGEL LINARES

C.ª S JERONIMO 48 Y PZA. DE LAS CORTES, 11
MADRID   TEL. 221 46 27

PLAZA DE LA CATEDRAL, 7
PALMA DE MALLORCA   TEL. 21 72 19

CUADROS, TAPICE:
JOYAS, MUEBLE:
Y BROCADOS ANTIGUO:

MADRID (14), January 19th, 1974.

Sr. Mr. Stewart D. Saxe, Suite 615, 85 Richmond St. W., Toronto, Ca — Debe

	nada.	PESETAS	CTS.
1	Antique silver pointer	7.500	00
	Less 10% discount	750	00
	Net amount	6.750	00
		or $120.55	

We hereby certify that the above mentioned
item is over 100 years old.

ABELARDO LINARES, S.A.

AL:ia

ABELARDO LINARES, S. A.
ANTIGÜEDADES
Plaza de las Cortes,
Carrera San Jeronimo, 48
TEL. 221-14-99
MADRID

CUEVO
IMMIGRATION
DOUANES
IMMIGRATION
JAN 20 1974
MONTREAL
83

[22]

[23]

[24]

[25]

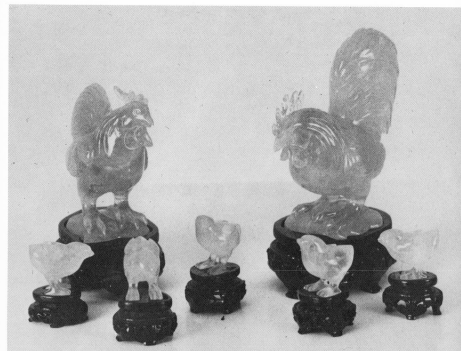

[26]

[27]

[28]

[29]

[30]

[31]

[32]

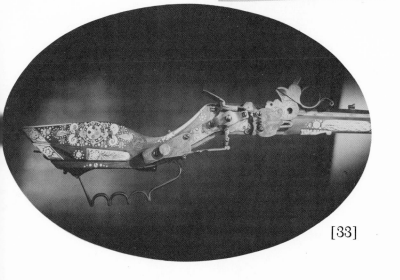

[33]

[34]

[35]

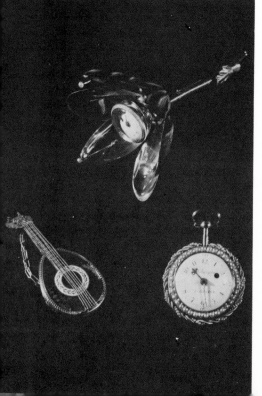

[36]

VI

WHEN

TO

SELL

The problems inherent in selling an art object are in some ways similar to those you encounter in selling a stock—when do you get out? With a stock you can look at the earnings, or the growth prospects, or the assets, and can then make a reasoned decision; but with a piece of art it is more difficult.

Boom-and-Bust Cycles

One absolute rule in selling art is to get out of an art field after it hits the front pages; that invariably indicates a peak has arrived. As an example I purchased a little Renoir at the Goldschmitt auction at Sotheby's in 1956 for $15,000; my purchase was followed by a boom in Impressionist art with a steady growth in value of the painting. Beginning in 1968, Japan experienced a wave of economic prosperity, and Japanese dealers went wild in their scramble to purchase Impressionist paintings for their businessmen clients. There were numerous articles on the front pages of *The New York Times* about the phenomenon— prices for Impressionists doubled and then tripled. In 1971 I sold my Renoir to a Japanese businessman for $85,000. (I paid a $7,500 commission to the dealer who brought us together.) Then in 1972 the bubble burst and prices collapsed: a painting similar to my Renoir sold at Parke Bernet last fall for $45,000. I managed to get out at the very top of the market!

Watch such cycles carefully, and when you notice that some large sector of the market is rushing to buy one kind of object, *sell*. Now hysteria has set in with another type of art—just as the Japanese celebrated their sudden prosperity by buying Renoirs, so the Arabs are spending their oil money on Eastern art: Oriental manuscripts, Middle Eastern paintings, and Arabian work of all kinds. This represents a once-in-a-lifetime opportunity for collectors in this field to get out at a huge profit, and the reason for it may not be far to seek. In England, where art prices are soaring because of the weakness of paper currency, "Arab money" is now praised or blamed for every new price rise in the art field. It has even gotten to the point where the phrase "Arab money" is greeted with a smile in the art world. When I used that phrase to one London dealer he replied, "It's more likely Russians with snow on their boots." I stared blankly at the man until he explained that this is an English phrase dating back to 1916 when there were rumors that Russian soldiers had landed in England to be used as reinforcements on the

Western front. People reported seeing thousands of these soldiers moving down to the channel and when they were asked how they knew they were Russians the answer was, "Because they had snow on their boots."

Despite my dealer friend's skepticism, the flood of Arab money is very real and is having a dramatic effect on every field of art which appeals to Arabic tastes. It certainly represents a wonderful opportunity to sell even second-rate pieces which two years ago could not be given away. The boom will not, of course, go on for ever (although the non-Arab world's dependence on Arab petroleum products would seem to guarantee a fairly lengthy bull market for Arabica); but use your eyes and your wits to predict similar market expansions for your benefit in the future. If certain groups or countries experience a wave of prosperity, they will cash in by buying into the art field. And if you want to sell what they want to buy, so much the better.

One of my friends just had a fantastic experience with the new Arab wealth. This man has collected old English silver for years, and his small but fine collection has moved up steadily in value. Last month a Toronto dealer phoned and told my friend that a buyer was in town from Kuwait and could she bring him to view the silver. Like most collectors my neighbor loves to show off his collection to other silver lovers, so he readily agreed. The Arab briefly examined the pieces and then said, "I would like to buy your collection—set a price." My neighbor laughed and said, "It's not really for sale." He added jokingly, "Everything in the house has a price, including my wife; but I would have to ask you a ridiculous amount." The visitor persisted, and my neighbor said, "$350,000." He had paid $16,000 in total for all the pieces and he considered that the collection was now worth between $150,000 and $200,000. To his utter shock the Arab said "Sold!" He returned the next day to pay for his purchase in $100 bills, setting only one condition on the sale—that neither the seller nor the dealer ever tell anyone who bought the collection.

The dazed dealer collected a $17,500 commission from each of them, and the totally mind-blown collector is now happily purchasing and building a new collection—this time it's Russian enamels, which appear to be of absolutely no interest to Arabs.

The Middle East buyers now coming into the market are relatively unsophisticated and tend to seek out the decorative end of the market—expensive jewelry pieces which they send not to Arabia but to their new homes in Paris or London. Calligraphy is considered in the Middle East to be the noblest of all the arts, and as a result prices of Islamic manuscripts have reached dizzy heights. Thus at Sotheby's this year *one single page* from a sixteenth-century book, *The Defeat of Hemu*, sold for an amazing $41,800.

Middle Eastern taste in paintings is quite different from ours (they love court portraits and have paid up to $500,-000 each), and they buy nineteenth- rather than eighteenth-century furniture almost exclusively, i.e., they are buying later attractive copies. The dealers joke about this, but I suspect that here at least the Arabs may be on the right track. It may well be that because eighteenth-century craftsmanship is so very good we have elevated it too much over that of the discredited nineteenth century. Remember that eighteenth-century pieces have all been carefully combed through, but there are still exciting discoveries to be made in nineteenth-century goods.

How do you become aware of current trends in prices, and how do you keep abreast of the approximate value of your art objects? An easy way to keep in touch is through a subscription to the Art Newsletter published by *Art News* at 750 Third Avenue, New York City. This biweekly report costs $60 per year and not only supplies information of art sale prices across the world but also tells which paintings failed to sell at auction and had to be bought in. I find it both enjoyable and useful, and I would no more be without it than I would be without the *Wall Street Journal*.

Also of great value is the *Art Investment Guide* published quarterly from Pond House, Weybridge, Surrey, England at £7.50 per year. This magazine gives in-depth studies of price trends in various art fields and is both a bargain and a must for the serious investor.

Sometimes an inside tip will give you the signal to sell. One such hint—which I will share with you—concerns Chinese snuff bottles made of jade and other semiprecious stones. They are certainly beautiful, and they command a very fancy price right now. But I happen to know that the

Chinese have a whole warehouse full of snuff bottles (between 80,000 and 100,000 of them) which they are planning to sell soon on the open market. When these objects are dumped in this manner, the price will collapse. So if you have any Chinese snuff bottles, sell them now.

Despite my vigilance for factors of this kind, I haven't always been as wise or successful in my sales as I was with my Renoir, largely because impatience led me to sell at the wrong time and for the wrong reasons. At A La Vieille Russie in New York in 1955 I discovered a sixteenth-century clock surmounted by an enormous ostrich and a bear carrying a drum, and I bought it from them for $5,000. My wife thought it was the ugliest object she had ever seen; worse, the flopping of the ostrich's wings and the bear's beating of the drum terrified my two-year-old son. In 1959 I succumbed and persuaded the store to buy the clock back from me at cost. Then in 1967 dealer Edgar Mannheimer in Zurich bought the clock for $160,000 and resold it to a client at some higher figure. Today it is in the Württemberg Museum in Stuttgart.

I did not do much better with my venture into Fabergé. In 1956 I bought a beautiful Fabergé table clock for $5,000 and resold it four years later, purely through ignorance and a temporary shortage of funds, for the same price. Today it is worth at least $40,000.

I lost a great deal of money on these two transactions simply because I was impatient. I sold the clock not because I was skeptical of its value but because someone else didn't like it—*never* a good reason for a sale. The most important rule in selling art is to wait until the right opportunity arises, and *not* to sell when you're under any kind of pressure.

Mannheimer recognized this; he knew the clock was worth much more than I had paid for it. He paid thirty-two times as much as I did and still made money on the deal because he was able to sell at leisure.

Nonspeculative Selling

Sometimes you should sell a work of art even though its price may not have reached its peak. At these times you should pay less attention to value fluctuations and more attention to other indicators. One of these is your personal taste. If you love a painting and looking at it gives you pleasure every day, you shouldn't sell it no matter how many front-page stories are written about the artist who painted it. On the other hand, when that same painting ceases to please it doesn't matter who painted it— if the price is right, sell it.

Another nonspeculative indicator to watch for is a recession, a so-called bear market, or a depression. It is important to remember that the value of works of art does not go down nearly as badly as that of stocks or real estate during market crashes. During the great depression when U.S. Steel sold at $1 and Abitibi Paper went to 5¢, established works of art continued to sell at or near their 1920 prices. Similarly, in 1970 when the new issue stock market collapsed in New York there was barely a ripple in the prices received at the international art auction sales. What this means is that sometimes in depressed periods you should consider cashing in your art profits rather than selling other items at great losses.

Sometimes a sale is dictated by the demands of your collection. It is a sad fact that none of us have enough money to buy all the things we might desire, and on occasion you will want to add something to your collection that you simply can't afford. This is the time to weed out your minor pieces and sell them; with the proceeds of their sale you can then buy the object you've been wanting.

The rule to follow here is: Constantly try to upgrade. Sell your mediocre pieces to buy better things, because the finest items in every field are the ones that have the biggest price advances in any boom. My two Rembrandt etchings exemplified this—my minor example of a portrait of the artist's mother cost me $20 and is now worth $800, but the finer one (Figure 23) cost $40 and is worth over $7,000. You will always do better financially by buying the best.

Blue-Chip Art

There is never a good time to sell blue-chip art— historical paintings and old masters' paintings, drawings, and graphics. On the other hand there is never a *bad* time to sell them. Their values move up steadily over the years. I bought my two Rembrandt etchings in 1952 for a total of $60. In 1971 I almost sold them for $1,800. This year I turned down an offer of $8,000. The same situation applies to Krieghoff. Between 1952 and 1958 I bought nine Krieghoff paintings for a total of $25,000 and resold eight of them in 1969 for $85,000. Today they would bring at least double that figure. So if you get any old masters' paintings or lithographs, hang onto them—unless, of course, you *have* to sell them. If and when that happens, you should take care to sell them where you will get the best possible price, a subject we will look into in the next chapter.

VII

WHERE
AND HOW
TO SELL

The sale of my Krieghoffs (see below) illustrates a number of basic rules in cashing in. First of all it is probably wiser to sell through an auction house—dealers are just too knowledgeable for you to be able to bargain intelligently, and there is too great a chance of being taken. Also, many dealers mark their objects up by over 100 percent, and it seems foolish to me to sell a painting to a gallery for $5,000 which they will resell for $10,000 a few weeks later.

There is one advantage to selling through a dealer, especially if you need cash in a hurry. A dealer will usually pay you right away—although some dealers will suggest that you leave your goods on consignment, saying they will pay you if and when they sell. I don't ever recommend this course because too many collectors have had difficulty collecting afterward. Insist on payment in full, and don't hesitate to ask for more than it is worth—the dealer will offer less and there is nothing wrong with bargaining under the circumstances. If you need a good appraisal of the worth of your goods, you are best off taking them to an auctioneer for a valuation. It commits you to nothing.

Selling at Auction

The best way to sell any work of art (if it is valuable) is through an auction house. I would use one of the auction galleries mentioned previously for they stand head and shoulder above all others: Parke Bernet in New York City, at 980 Madison Avenue, and—in London—Sotheby's, at 34 New Bond Street, W1, and Christie's, at 8 King Street, SW 1. There are quite literally hundreds of other auctioneers in North America, but practically all of them are small galleries selling local, inexpensive articles; none of them attract the big international sellers or buyers. Also unfortunately, almost all these small auctioneers mix their own objets d'art in with the customers' art, and too many of them use shills and sell defective or fake material.

These dangers are nonexistent at the big three. Their catalogs go to every corner of the earth, and an important sale can attract thousands of bidders and tens of thousands of bids. What's more, they stand behind everything they sell and as a result they get larger bids and more bidders.

Don't be afraid that if you put a painting up for auction someone will be able to get it for a preposterously low price—any reputable auctioneer will allow you to place a "reserve" bid on your art objects so that no disastrously low prices are received. In Sotheby's sale of my Krieghoffs they suggested reserve bids totaling $80,000 on the seven paintings which had cost me $25,000 ten years earlier. This proved very astute advice; although the sale went well and took in over $85,000, one of the paintings inexplicably received no bids and would have gone for a song if the reserve had not been there to protect it.

Everyone—not just dealers and established collectors— has access to the big three auctioneers; for a 10- to 20- percent commission they will happily handle the sale of anything that is old and valuable. And of course you do not have to sell a whole collection in order to use an auction house. If you have only one or two pieces of value to offer, the auctioneer will include them with other material from other sellers in order to make up a sale. There is only one restriction: if your collection is modern you will probably have to depend on dealers. (This is one more reason to avoid modern art—the big auctioneers just will not touch much of it, there being no resale market for too much of it.)

Once you have brought your collection to the auction house, the auctioneer will inspect your pieces. If at this point the auction house feels that any object is of inferior quality (or, worse yet, a worthless forgery), they will refuse to sell that object. If the object passes inspection, the auctioneer will appraise it and will recommend a reserve bid. These reserves are negotiable, both as to size and the commission, if any, to be paid if the items *don't* sell. There is no fixed figure here—the auction house must cover its costs but if the sale is big enough it will often be willing to waive commission on any articles that do not sell. Furthermore, if your collection is worth a lot of money (anything over $50,000) the commission on the whole lot becomes negotiable, so it is worthwhile contacting two of the houses. Sotheby's and Parke Bernet are under the same ownership, so you should talk to one of them and to Christie's. The higher the value of your collection the lower the commission you have to pay; it can be as low as 10 percent or as high as 25 percent.

When the auctioneer has appraised your collection and you have set whatever reserves you decide on, the auction house will often advance you some of the cash you expect to realize from the sale (it may be weeks or even months before the auction proper takes place). Selling at auction —especially through the big houses—is not a process that provides instant gratification; but it is the surest way to maximize the profit on your art investments.

Selling Independently

There are ways of handling a sale other than through dealers or auctions, and one of these is the private sale to other collectors. You can reach them through an ad in an antique or art magazine or by attending one of the conventions of the art specialty you have collected.

A few art investors have become so deeply involved in their hobby and/or investment that when they finally decide to sell out they are able to do so professionally. One gentleman opened a shop in Toronto which he called the Real and Rare Gallery and from which he is selling out his personal collection of Oriental art at retail prices. Another investor hired a booth at the New York antique fair and got rid of his collection in one week of hectic sales.

And if your collection is in a specific field you can always approach one or more of the leading collectors in that field directly. They are always happy to hear from private sellers so they too can avoid dealer's commissions or auction fees.

Last May the Art Newsletter compiled the following list of the world's leading collectors with their specialties:

Giovanni Agnelli, Turin, Fiat fortune: Impressionist and early twentieth-century art.

James Alsdorf, Chicago, manufacturing executive: antiquities, twentieth-century art.

Harry W. Anderson, San Francisco, vice-president of Saga Food Corporation: contemporary art.

Walter H. Annenberg, Wynnewood, Pa., president, Triangle Publications: Impressionist and post-Impressionist art.

Audrey Beck, Houston, late husband John owned *Houston Chronicle:* Impressionist and post-Impressionist art.

Edwin Bergman, Chicago, chairman of U.S. Reduction Corporation: Surrealist art.

Leigh Block, Chicago, director of Inland Steel: Impressionist art.

Mrs. Harry L. Bradley, Milwaukee, late husband was electronics manufacturer: contemporary art.

B. Gerald Cantor, Beverly Hills, investment banker: sculpture, nineteenth- and twentieth-century paintings.

Edward William Carter, Los Angeles, chairman of Carter Hawley Hale Stores, Inc.: old masters (particularly Dutch).

Marchioness of Cholmondeley, London, Sassoon family wealth, worldwide investments: eighteenth-century French art.

Douglas Cooper, Argilliers, France, real estate: nineteenth- and twentieth-century art.

Nathan Cummings, New York, retired chairman of Consolidated Foods Corporation: nineteenth- and twentieth-century paintings.

Georges Embericos, Lausanne, shipping: Cézanne, van Gogh, modern masters.

Mahmoud Foroughi, Tehran, former Iranian ambassador to the United States: Islamic art.

Edgar W. and Bernice Garbisch, New York; he is a former corporation executive, she is the daughter of Walter Chrysler, Sr.: Impressionist and American folk art.

John Goelet, Paris, real estate: old masters.

Basil Goulandris, Paris, Greek shipping, Impressionist and post-Impressionist art.

Joseph Hirshhorn, Naples, Fla., chairman of Callahan Mining Company: nineteenth- and twentieth-century art.

Seward Johnson, Princeton, N.J., Johnson & Johnson: old masters and modern art.

Alice M. Kaplan, New York, wife of Jacob M. Kaplan, former president of Welch's Grape Juice Company: antiquities and nineteenth- and twentieth-century American art.

Gilbert Kinney, Washington, D.C., former foreign service officer: modern American art.

David Lloyd Kreeger, Washington, D.C., chairman and chief executive officer, Government Employees Insurance Co.: Impressionist and post-Impressionist art.

Pierre Levy, Paris, textiles: Fauve and early twentieth-century French art.

Jack and Belle Linsky, New York; he is the chairman of Swingline Staples: old masters and nineteenth- and twentieth-century art.

Peter Ludwig, Aachen, chocolate manufacturer: medieval and modern art.

Imelda Marcos, Philippines, mayor of Manila and wife of president: contemporary art.

Morton D. May, St. Louis, May department stores: South Pacific and German Expressionist art.

Alistair McAlpine, London, contractor: twentieth-century art.

Henry P. McIlhenny, Philadelphia, trolley fortune: nineteenth-century French art, eighteenth- and nineteenth-century English and Irish art.

Algur H. Meadows, Dallas, oil company executive: Spanish art, contemporary art.

Paul Mellon, Upperville, Va., financier: English sporting paintings, Impressionist and twentieth-century art.

Domenique de Menil, Houston, late husband John was chairman of Schlumberger, Ltd., oil drilling equipment company: twentieth-century art.

Stavros Spyros Niarchos, London, Greek shipping: Impressionist and post-Impressionist art.

Giuseppe Panza, Milan, chemicals: contemporary art.

Ted Power and son Alan, London, television, hi-fi radio: 1950s and '60s art.

Joseph Pulitzer, Jr., St. Louis, editor and publisher, *St. Louis Post-Dispatch:* twentieth-century art and modern masters.

David Rockefeller, New York, president, Chase Manhattan Bank: nineteenth- and twentieth-century European art.

John D. Rockefeller III, New York, philanthropist, financier: Oriental and nineteenth-century art.

Nelson Rockefeller, New York: eclectic.

Lessing J. Rosenwald, Jenkintown, Pa., former chairman, Sears, Roebuck and Co.: prints.

Robert Rowan, Pasadena, real estate: American postwar art, particularly Californian.

Habib Sadet, Tehran, businessman and banker: nineteenth- and twentieth-century art.

Robert Sainsbury, London, supermarkets: African and modern art.

Harold Samuels, London, real estate: Dutch old masters and modern art.

Norbert Schimmel, New York, printing equipment: antiquities and Oriental art.

Norton Simon, Los Angeles, business executive: eclectic.

Howard Sirak, Columbus, Ohio, surgeon: Impressionist and twentieth-century art.

Robert Smith, Bethesda, Md., real estate: Dutch old masters and twentieth-century American art.

Baron Heinrich Thyssen, Lugano, industrialist, former president, Thyssengas and Niederrheinische Gas und Wasserwerke: old masters and modern art.

Robert Tobin, San Antonio, aerial survey, set designs: contemporary American paintings, Impressionist art.

Emily and Burton Tremaine, Meriden, Conn., manufacturing: early twentieth-century art.

Joseph Wohl, New York, real estate: Impressionist and twentieth-century art.

Virginia and Bagley Wright, Seattle, lumber: contemporary art.

Charles Wrightsman, Palm Beach, Fla., oil: eclectic.

Death and Taxes

The collector who sells art at a profit must pay taxes on that profit; fortunately, however, these taxes come primarily in the form of capital gains tax, which swallows a much smaller percentage of your profit than ordinary income tax does. The definition of a "capital gain" can be simple or complex, depending on what country you're in. In Canada, for example, capital gains tax applies whenever something is bought and sold at a profit. In the United States, the situation is more complicated. Up until

1976, your profits from an art sale could qualify as a capital gain if the object sold had been in your possession for six months, but that requirement has been changed to nine months for 1977 and will be further changed to twelve months in 1978. The amount of tax that you pay will vary vastly, however, depending on whether you are an art *collector* or an art *investor*—the two terms may sound similar, but they are tremendously different.

An art collector is defined as anyone who puts only a relatively small proportion of his capital into art objects— he makes purchases primarily for the pleasure of ownership. If you are a collector and you sell one of your treasures, you cannot deduct the cost of art insurance, repairs, or storage from your taxable capital gain; nor can you deduct from your income any loss on the sale of an unsuccessful purchase. You do not have the right to exchange your art for other art pieces without paying full capital gains tax—swapping is not tax free, even if not a cent changes hands.

Things get worse for the collector's heirs (financially, at least) if he dies. It used to be that if a painting was bought for $10,000 and appreciated to $100,000, the heirs would pay estate tax on the increased value, at which point the painting was considered as having cost $100,000 and no further income tax was payable if it was sold at that figure. The United States tax reform act of December 1976 has changed all that; now your heirs pay estate tax on a $10,000 painting, and, when the painting is sold, full tax for the increased value—$100,000—will have to be paid. (Valuation goes only as far back as December 1976, so any gain prior to that is exempt.) The situation was neatly summed up by Eugene Vogel, the New York lawyer and tax expert: "This makes death less desirable than it used to be."

For tax purposes the art investor is immeasurably better off than the collector—insurance and storage costs can be deducted from his income, as can art magazine subscriptions; losses can be taken, and in certain cases even depreciation is allowable. The only difficulty the investor is likely to run into is that involved in convincing the government that he is an art investor and not just a collector. If you're really serious about making money from your art purchases, it's worth taking the trouble to convince them; all you need to show is that your primary purpose is investment and not personal enjoyment. You can do this by showing that (1) a significant proportion of your capital is invested in art as compared to other forms of investment; (2) you have complete records of your purchases and sales; (3) much of your art is not on display in your home; and (4) you have received the advice of experts in your buying. If you follow these rules you will save tens of thousands of dollars when the time comes to sell.

"Selling" for a Tax Break

There is one method of selling which most investors overlook although it is an absolutely certain way of making a profit—donate your art to your local museum or gallery. In the art market, it is truly blessed to give!

This method is not only profitable but will also make you locally popular and can even give you a measure of immortality. After all, it's rather nice to have your name on the wall of the Metropolitan Museum as one of its patrons.

Governments find it very difficult to justify the appropriation of funds for our public cultural institutions so they get money to them by the back door—by giving tax credits to persons who make donations to those institutions. The mechanism is very simple, although it varies slightly from jurisdiction to jurisdiction. The donor presents an art object to a public gallery, the gallery issues a receipt for the value of the article, and the donor may then deduct the amount of the receipt from his income tax. The total amount deductible from an individual's income varies depending on the area and the individual's tax bracket; but generally speaking art gift deductions are limited to 30 percent of your net income. (Gifts of larger size can be carried forward for up to five years, with one caveat—if you die, the tax credit disappears and cannot be used by your heirs.)

If you wish to profit from art gift tax deductions there are two routes to follow. One is to invite the director of your local museum to view your collection and decide if there are any items which the institution would care to have. The objects must then be valued by at least two independent experts in order to satisfy the tax authorities. Whatever you do, *don't fool around with this requirement,* or you may find your tax deduction disallowed.

In the early nineteen-sixties there was so much hanky-panky going on in the United States in connection with grossly inflated appraisals of art gifts to charitable institutions that the U.S. Congress threatened to remove art donations from the tax exemption list entirely. In response to this the Art Dealers Association of America was formed to provide a fair appraisal service whose opinion the Internal Revenue Service could accept without doubt. The A.D.A. now appraises all works of art given to museums and in the past fourteen years has examined a total of $300,000,000 worth of art. In doing their appraisals they set value on the basis of what a willing buyer would pay a willing seller when both are aware of all the relevant facts. But no matter who does your appraising, make sure you follow four rules:

(1) Beware of the general appraiser who advertises himself as an expert in all art fields; anyone who claims to be able to appraise everything probably can't appraise anything. An expert can only be expert in a very limited field—it takes too many years to learn the specifics.

(2) Remember that not everything goes up. Ninety-nine percent of the paintings and art objects created in any single year decline in value and most of them have no resale value.

(3) Don't accept all appraisals unquestioningly. Any valuation is just an informed estimate—each work of art is unique and its value will vary depending on its size, its medium, its condition, and its quality. Get a confirming opinion.

(4) Be absolutely sure that the art work is actually the work of the artist who is supposed to have created it. It has been said that Rembrandt painted seven hundred pic-

tures, of which three thousand are in America; don't be foolish and attempt to donate a worthless fake.

The second method of profiting from your tax deductions is to approach any museum and ask them what objects they are looking for. Every museum and gallery is always on the lookout for items to enrich its collections, and they are happy to tell you of any specific objects they would like to own. You then purchase these objects and put them in your home and enjoy them for a few years while the wonders of inflation push up their value. After a few years (in the United States the figure is six years) you give the art objects to the museum and take your tax deduction—which by that time is certain to be high enough to cover your costs and give you a profit—and start all over again with new art objects.

There can be one complication to this route—capital gains tax; so check with your accountant about the local, state, and federal laws. Generally speaking, the United States government waives capital gains tax on such gifts if the object has been in your possession for six years, and in Canada capital gains tax can be avoided by giving your gift under Bill C33, which not only gives complete exemption from capital gains but also allows an individual to deduct up to 100 percent of his income and pay no tax at all.

Since capital gains tax must be paid on profitable cash sales of art just as on profitable sales of stocks, bonds, or any other investment, the charitable gift route of selling can work out to be much more profitable than actually selling the art for money: if you have a large capital gain a sale will net you only 60 percent of the proceeds after taxes while a gift will net 70 percent if you are in a high tax bracket.

Be careful, however, with gifts to tax-exempt charitable institutions other than museums, for the Internal Revenue Service has ruled that you can receive this full tax deduction only "if the recipient uses the gift in its exempt function." What this means is that a gift of a painting to be given to your local church and auctioned off is *not* deductible. Take care to ensure that your charity really wants the gift and will show it on its walls—otherwise you may lose both your donation and your deduction. And, as Eugene Vogel pointed out in a speech on October 30, 1976, to the World Art Market Conference, don't demand that the gallery give you a written undertaking that they will never sell; this makes your donation a "restricted" gift, and only "unrestricted" gifts are fully deductible.

Giving away your art acquisitions also offers an easy— and often profitable—way out if you've made a mistake in your buying. In the huge collection of Chinese crafts that I purchased in its entirety (see page 46) was an amazing once-in-a-lifetime piece: an extraordinary conglomeration consisting of the hundred-year-old cloisonné vase placed on a modern gold cart and covered with a gold canopy, pulled by a golden stag, the whole studded with turquoise and coral. It is literally priceless and could never be reproduced.

Unfortunately this is a rather large piece—it is over two feet high—and I couldn't figure out quite what to do with it! I have a large home but nowhere was there space for this overwhelming and precious object. I "temporarily" placed it on our dining room table where it rested majestically for eight glorious weeks; we even had a dinner party and used it as the centerpiece, but we found that our guests couldn't see each other because of its size. Finally my wife rebelled and ordered that I get rid of "that monstrosity" on pain of some horrible alternatives. It was so enormous and so impossible to display that I couldn't sell it, but that didn't mean I had to suffer. I gave it to the Ontario Heritage Foundation, for a suitable tax write-off, and it is now on exhibit at the Royal Ontario Museum.

You can even use this method to "profit" from pieces you *don't* want to get rid of. If you are attached to a work of art and don't want to part with it, you can still make money on it by giving it to a museum or gallery with the provision that it remain in your possession until your death. This way you get an immediate tax deduction but continue to get pleasure from that art object as long as you live. The galleries are happy to go along with this method because they know that sooner or later they will get the gift and it will be even more valuable by that time.

Another excellent way of handling such a gift is to give it physically to the museum and take your tax deduction but have the museum give you an option to purchase back the gift *at the same price* at any time during your lifetime or that of your children. This allows you to get your immediate tax deduction and if inflation continues to roar away will also allow you to buy the art objects back at some future date at practically no cost. This is not such a pleasant prospect for the museum, which will be forced to hold on to the objects even if it would rather sell or trade them; so you can only use this method with important or rare objects which the museum is very anxious to have.

That, of course, is the operative principle, as I've stressed time and time again. Buy the best—buy what *you* like, what other people want, and what you know to be outstanding. If you start by buying wisely, selling wisely is always easy.

VIII

FINAL
PRECAUTIONS

The great disadvantage in investing in art rather than real property or stock is that some thief may steal your investment; therefore it is essential to protect yourself with insurance. Art theft is epidemic. The head of New York's burglary squad estimated that in 1976 art theft ranked just behind the illegal traffic in narcotics in international crime and that the total value of art stolen could be as much as a billion dollars in a year!

A surprising number of my friends who have substantial holdings in silver, paintings, and other easily portable art have not insured their collections but depend solely on their security system. Very elaborate and relatively inexpensive methods are now available to protect one's home, including guard dogs, noise alarms, or silent alarms connected to local police stations. It is an unfortunate fact that no system has been devised which cannot be breached by a determined, expert thief. Some collectors put their faith in the fame of their pieces or of the artists involved, believing that certain paintings are internationally known and would be recognized anywhere as stolen. But many of them have learned to their sorrow that that is no protection, for a number of thefts have taken place in recent years purely and simply for ransom. Thus in January 1976 a French gallery was held up and 149 Picassos were stolen at gunpoint, even though there was never any thought of attempting to sell them.

When an art theft takes place the police of the locality in which the theft occurred immediately send a bulletin with a photograph of the missing object all over the world. It is a depressing fact that a very high percentage of these bulletins achieve absolutely no result, and many thefts go unsolved. One of the largest took place in Moscow in 1975, when art collector George Costakis, owner of Moscow's best-known private art collection, was robbed of more than 1,000 paintings worth over two million dollars. At first the Soviets gave the crime no publicity, but they finally released the news when they concluded that the art had been smuggled out of the U.S.S.R.

This theft has completely baffled Interpol. The works are practically all by contemporary Soviet painters, and as the investigating officer put it, "Why would anyone want them? They can't be sold; they can't be ransomed and they are too ugly to hang!"

Insurance

There can be only one real security for art investment and that is insurance. The cost is minuscule (less than one half of 1 percent per year in most localities) and anyone who has made a sizeable investment is extremely foolish if he doesn't protect himself in this way. You can reduce your insurance cost by taking elementary precautions. I received a one-third reduction in my insurance bill by keeping my automata watches in a safe except when they are on show rather than leaving them on display in my home.

The value of insurance was borne home to me one summer morning in 1969 when I came downstairs to find my collection of paintings by Cornelius Krieghoff gone while nothing else had been disturbed.

Two well-briefed thieves had breached my security system, avoided our guard dog, and come through the only unwired window in the house to steal them. The most elaborate precautions had not protected my paintings— but fortunately they were insured.

There is little respect for thieves among insurance companies, and when the robbers rather trustingly opened negotiations with the insurer that company sent along three policemen to do the negotiating. The paintings were recovered and the thieves got ten years, during which they can ponder the unreliability of insurance companies.

It doesn't always work out that well. The greatest problem is the statute of limitations, which provides that after a certain number of years a crime ceases to be a crime. Thus from three to ten years after a theft (depending on the country—it is seven years in the United States) the person found with stolen art can no longer be charged with stealing that art, and in most countries after thirty years the owner of the stolen art object loses his claim of ownership.

103

During World War II, in fact, entire collections of price-less art were stolen by the Germans in France and later by the Allies in Germany. The thirty years' limit has now expired and supposedly "lost" pieces are now reappearing at the auction houses all over the world—and there is nothing the former owners can do about it. Because of this law, sophisticated criminals now routinely store valu-able hot art objects in bank vaults for the required seven years and then ship them to Switzerland for sale at auc-tion.

There is only one situation in which insurance may not be a necessity but an extravagance.

If the art investor has a painting stolen or destroyed, he may deduct from his regular income either the original cost or the current market value, whichever is less. If the investor is in a high income-tax bracket, and if the stolen object has been recently purchased (which means that the original cost and the current market value are virtually identical), he may deduct its full value from his income— and the government ends up paying 70 percent of the loss. Individuals in such situations are probably just as well off not insuring these objects, but for most people this is not really a practical consideration.

What it boils down to is that there is only one real protection against loss of your investment: Insurance!

IX

A MASTER PLAN
FOR THE
BEGINNING INVESTOR

Now the time has come for the nitty-gritty—a master plan for the beginning collector who is starting an investment career in art in 1977.

Most people reading this book will have had some experience in investing through the purchase of stocks, bonds, or a home—many may even have purchased paintings or other art objects for aesthetic purposes, but very few will have bought an art piece for investment. So I have set up a scenario for those important initial purchases —it's time to start to make money. As a guide I will describe how I began a new collection just one year ago.

Getting Your Feet Wet

I have been vaguely aware of Russian enamels for many years and actually bought a few modern pieces for gifts when I was on a trip to the U.S.S.R. nine years ago. The spoons and small cups cost $10 to $15 each, they were small and easily carried and I brought them home, gave them away and forgot about them.

Exactly one year ago I was browsing on Fifth Avenue in New York and noticed in the window of a shop at the corner of Forty-seventh Street an ornate, heavily worked enamel and silver spoon in a mélange of blues, reds, yellows, and golds. It was gaudy but terribly rich looking.

I went into the shop and examined the piece—the price on it was $75 and the date 1902 was stamped into the handle. The price *seemed* to be O.K., but I really didn't have a clue as to the value of such items. I didn't know whether they were rare or common, and I had no idea how to tell if this piece was real or fake. So I thanked the salesman and left the store thinking that I might have stumbled onto a new field of investment—or that I had just examined a pretty but worthless piece of merchandise.

Actually, at this point, I had already fulfilled three of the basic rules in art investment:

(1) The pieces appealed to my aesthetic sense—they were beautiful to my eyes. There are so many different kinds and styles of art objects that it would be utter folly to invest in a form that doesn't give you emotional pleasure. As I've said time and again during the course of this book, this first rule must be satisfied before I even think about whether the object meets the other requirements.

(2) The enamels were in my price range. For an initial investment only $75 was required, and at that level I knew that I would have no difficulty in gradually assembling a substantial collection. This too is obviously essential, for

it is usually an error to buy into a field which is so expensive that you will be unable to add to your initial purchases. A collection of similar objects will always sell at a better price than single odd pieces, unless you are trying to sell one important painting or an object of like value— something you're unlikely to do as a beginning investor.

(3) I also already knew that there was a lot of similar material about—I had been casually looking at it for years —so I would have little difficulty in acquiring more pieces in this field.

Now I took the first serious step to develop my initial interest. I went to the library and looked up the file on Russian enamels and was delighted to discover that there were dozens of books on the subject. This fulfilled my next rule:

(4) There must be comprehensive written material available in that particular art field. I borrowed half a dozen of the more recent books and spent the weekend learning about enamels, their history, how they are made, where they were made, how many were turned out and where most of them ended up. As it turned out these enamel pieces had all been made in Russia, the good pieces were all done prior to 1917, there had been a huge amount produced for the well-to-do, and as a result of the Russian revolution the pieces had been scattered all over the world.

I was sold and became terribly excited. This was obviously a direction from which I was going to gain both pleasure and profit. You might think that at this point I went rushing back to the original dealer and bought the spoon that had started me on my quest. But I didn't. *Never* act hastily once you think you know what you want. Be patient. In this case my next step was to find out what Russian enamels were worth and where was the best place to buy, so on Monday morning I went over to Parke Bernet on Madison Avenue and asked how often they had sales of Russian enamels and when the next one would take place. The clerk told me that the sales took place several times each year and that the next one would be in two weeks. I purchased the catalog for $2 and went home to study the prices.

(5) That particular sale featured 513 different lots covering the entire range of Russian enamels from Easter eggs to matchbox holders, from spoons to an entire service—the sight of all those beautiful pieces, at what were very low prices compared to other fields of silver with which I was familiar, boggled my mind. Now I was beginning to understand values in this field.

(6) So I set out to pick a dealer's brains. I went back to my original shop on Fifth Avenue and purchased the spoon. This purchase, which I now knew was a good value, also established my good faith with the dealer. *Now* I could ask him questions that I couldn't ask before becoming a "client." I told the dealer quite honestly that I had never purchased anything like the spoon before, knew nothing about it, and would he please advise me of its history, where these things sold, and of the danger of fakes.

(7) I was relieved to learn that fakery is not a problem in this field for two reasons: first, much of the old art of

enameling has been lost and modern enamelers cannot duplicate the old pieces, and second, even if someone knew how to do it, to make a copy would cost more than the original sells for.

In other art fields two objects might look alike superficially, but if a dealer thinks that one is authentic and the other dubious he will consult with other dealers, auction houses, or museums. There is no reason the private collector can't do the same. It costs nothing.

(8) I was now truly assured of my piece's quality—an important point. In this field *as in all other art investments* the prime factor in resale value of any individual object is its quality. What is quality? It is a word that connotes the fineness of work in a particular piece, as well as the way it compares with other similar works. Is the piece damaged? Can the damage be repaired? Will the repair show? All of these will affect value.

(9) I was also reassured about my piece's authenticity— without having to ask for a certification. Don't pay too much attention to certificates of authenticity—an amazing number are phony. If you buy from a reputable dealer or auction house you don't need a certificate, and if the dealer is not reputable the certificate is worthless. If you have bought from a good dealer he will have carefully checked the item before he bought it. If it turns out the item is a fake the dealer will not have to be persuaded to buy it back. On the contrary, he will want it back at once—it represents the worst possible publicity for him.

Fortunately, certificates are declining both in number and in relative importance. Remember, any honest dealer hesitates to give certificates—dishonest dealers will give them freely.

(10) Once you have established your interest in a particular kind of art, you will want to go on and buy more pieces, as I did. How do you know what to pay for them? On December 10, 1976, a beautiful Easter egg was coming up for sale at Parke Bernet and I wanted to buy it, but first I had to establish what it was worth. I visited several of the New York dealers handling these eggs and found that they were priced from $3,000 to $4,000 but of course as an investor I expected to pay much less. Parke Bernet suggested a price of about $1,500 to $2,500, but the best guide turned out to be the prices received at a similar sale held in London only a few weeks before, where a replica of the egg both as to size and condition sold for only $1,200. I bid $1,300. It is essential for the art investor to subscribe to the catalogs and prices paid at Sotheby's, Christie's, and Parke Bernet; they cost only a few dollars a year for each art specialty and without them you are buying blind.

I am now well along in my collection of Russian enamels —I have thirteen spoons, a sugar tong, a compact, an egg, a chalice, and a cup—and although each purchase was made separately the collection looks like a unit. I love their color and beauty; but most important—and this is what it's all about—in the one year since I started collecting, Russian enamels have gone up 15 to 20 percent in price. Do you have *any* investment that did better in 1976?

By now you're probably wondering where to find investment values in art if you're not interested in Russian enamels. What, specifically, should you put your money in? Obviously not automata watches or Impressionist paintings—the prices are now far too high for investment purposes. You must seek out the beautiful objects that have been overlooked by the speculators during this past hectic inflationary decade. And you'll find that there are still many opportunities. As Peter Wilson, the chairman of Sotheby's, once advised, "In financial terms there is more fun to be had in buying inexpensively before a rise in market values than in outbidding the big buyers when the market is at its peak."* There is also more profit in it— so look for objects of a kind that have not undergone huge price advances.

Start with Less Than $500

The main thing to remember about buying art is that you don't need a lot of money to start. The art market is one of the last places where you can begin investing with as little as a few hundred dollars and still have a reasonable chance of outstanding success. In contrast this has not been true of the stock market since 1969: commodity brokers demand a minimum $5,000 initial investment; bags of silver coins cost $2,000 or more, and the smallest bond denomination is $1,000.

Yet art is so diversified both as to range of objects and values that the beginner with only a few dollars can still

* *Antiques International* (New York: Putnam, 1967.)

buy an object of beauty which will not only grow in value over the years but which will begin paying instant dividends in the form of beauty and pleasure. As I mentioned earlier, Russian enamels represent an excellent investment. Last year I purchased a Russian enamel-and-silver spoon (Figure 24) in a Toronto antique shop for $80. Made before the First World War in Leningrad (then St. Petersburg), these spoons were handmade but were turned out by the thousands and so are still available at very modest prices. At the Miami Antique Show in January 1976 there were dozens of these spoons and other utensils of this type offered for sale; many were far more elaborately decorated than my sample, but even the most beautiful sold for a maximum of $300. They are bound to increase in price as the flight from paper money accelerates.

Beautiful enamelware is still being manufactured in the Soviet Union; it is sold at very modest prices and makes a nice modest investment, but there should be little difficulty telling the modern from the old. The antique ware is far richer, more detailed and intricate.

For the investor with more funds available, similar sets of enameled Russian utensils are available for anywhere from $500 to $2,000, and there is a further dividend—the pleasure of use added to those of investment and joy of beauty. There is a very special feeling in drinking tea from a hundred-and-fifty-year-old service, imagining the family of Russian aristocrats, served by a retinue of serfs, in their villa outside Moscow, who might have used it originally.

Buying What's New

Not everything you buy need be an antique; price tags are naturally much lower on objects produced in the recent past. The trick here is to figure out which of the thousands of contemporary art objects will retain its value, or increase in value, as it in turn becomes old and an antique. I believe that in the field of painting this is impossible—there are just too many painters and the odds are too high against any one. But in certain other fields you have a better chance because you can buy an object for its utilitarian value and the investment opportunity is a bonus. A perfect example is a watch manufactured by the Arnex Watch Company in Switzerland and imported for U.S. distribution through its Manhattan headquarters.

The original model for this watch was made in Geneva in 1802; water flows from a fountain, a horse lowers his head to drink, and a falconer raises and lowers his arm while music plays in the background. The watch was purchased by a German Jewish collector in Berlin in 1931; during the war it was confiscated by the Nazis and ended up, in 1944, in the collection of Herman Goering. In 1946 an American officer "liberated" the watch and sold it in Paris to a dealer, who in turn sold it to Egypt's King Farouk. In 1954, Farouk fled to Italy, and General Naguib ordered the auctioning of Farouk's art collection; this watch was purchased by a Swiss collector. In 1970 the owner of Arnex got the brilliant idea of making a modern copy of the watch and he succeeded remarkably well—

the watch parts are modern and entirely different from the original but the automata moving figures are exact copies. The watch is turned out in small numbers and retails for about $500 in U.S. jewelry stores, and at that price the purchaser certainly gets his money's worth. It has all the advantages of a modern watch, is a beautiful conversation piece in addition, and is a pretty fair investment. (If you are planning a trip to Europe, the watch is available in Italy, Switzerland, and France—the price is about one-third less than in New York, but then you may have to pay import duty.)

Contemporary Chinese lacquerware is both attractive and—unlike its antique counterpart—inexpensive. A lovely tea set (Figure 25) can be purchased today in New York for about $100, and it is both a delight to the eye and a pleasure to use. The drawback in purchasing lacquer in North America is the huge duty added on by U.S. or Canadian customs—this same set can be purchased today in Peking department stores for $27 and is wholesaled at $18. If you get the opportunity to visit China or Hong Kong be sure to bring back some lacquer. Twenty years from now it will be looked upon as a valuable antique.

Among modern pottery the most beautiful and also, in my opinion, the best investment is the Satsuma ware of Japan. After glazing it is baked before the application of each color, with an additional baking after every coat. Finally, 24-karat gold is applied, baked on, and polished.

In Japan an outstanding coffee set in Satsuma ware sells for $70. Dinner services are priced from $200 to $1,000, and tea sets from $50 to $100. If one can ever be certain of a future collector's item, Satsuma surely fits the category.

Markups in the United States are horrendous, and this same coffee set may be priced at $500 on Fifth Avenue, so it is advisable to purchase directly from Japan. There are shops in Tokyo with large selections in most of the hotel shopping arcades, and you don't have to make a trip to Japan to buy. Write the Tokyo chamber of commerce and they will give you the names of several of these shops. It is cheaper to buy them by mail than it is to buy them here even after paying the import duty.

Another excellent initial investment for the would-be collector is rose quartz. Unlike other hardstones, such as jade, turquoise, or lapis lazuli, its price has not soared out of sight because it is not so rare. It is still possible to buy a fine set of carvings (Figure 26) for only $500; but do it now—the demand for these objects is growing steadily and the price is sure to increase over the next few years. One thing you should be careful of—rose quartz should only be purchased from a reputable dealer because poor crystal can easily be dyed temporarily. It is quite a shock to see the color fading away six months after its purchase!

Bargain Antiques and Antiquities

Finally, despite all I have said about investing in "recent" art objects, there is one very different type of investment that I should mention as a good start for a collection. The finest investments in the art field today are antiquities: they are beautiful, inexpensive, freely available, and easily resaleable. Thousands of ancient Syrian, Greek, and Roman glasses and pots have survived and can be purchased from reliable dealers like Spinks or at auction at Sotheby's or Christie's for anywhere from $100 to $500, depending on size, age, and condition. And besides its being beautiful and a good investment, it is very exciting to own a glass crafted before Christ's birth.

More recent, but still old, objects make good, low-priced investments. After paintings, furniture is the single most widely collected art object in the world.

Everyone has furniture and everyone needs it, and old furniture tends to be sold or passed on rather than junked. Furniture goes through several definite, graded steps from new to used to old to junk, until finally it becomes an antique. That very ugly Victorian chair which your grandmother treasured, your mother put in the attic, and you are now considering re-covering will be a valuable antique to your children. So if you need a table for your house or apartment, you are far better off buying a secondhand fifty-year-old wood table for the same $100 you would pay for a shiny brand-new plastic one. This is the one art field where age guarantees profits—there is no cheap old furniture. The dining room table on which I am writing this book is part of a set originally carved in 1873 for a wealthy Canadian family. It cost them $180 in 1873 dollars. I found the set in 1961 in a junkyard, and the owner was happy to sell the table and ten torn chairs for $200. It cost me $175 to re-cover the chairs. Value today is $4,500.

The eight beautiful varied objects listed in the last few pages can be individually purchased today for anywhere from $80 to $500 in New York City. The entire collection can be bought for $2,000, and I will guarantee huge and continued dividends in the form of pleasure and large cash profits to the person who holds on to them for a few years.

$500 and Up

For the collector who has more than a few hundred dollars to start out with, there are many more possibilities. Good investments in this category are icons, Chinese paintings, Tibetan art, Jewish marriage scrolls, Fabergé, old guns, and the like.

In the fall of 1916, Maria Feodorovna, the mother of Czar Nicholas of Russia, toured the hospitals behind the front in her function as head of the Russian Red Cross. As a gesture of appreciation the army presented her with a magnificent icon.

After the collapse of the government in 1917, Czarina Maria fled to the Crimea from which she and her daughter, the Grand Duchess Olga, escaped on a British warship to England. The Grand Duchess ended up living in a cottage in a small town in Ontario with a few mementoes from her luxurious past. After her death in 1962 I purchased one of her icons for $450 from her heirs (Figure 27).

Icons have gone up very little in price in the last twenty years in comparison with almost all other art, and a sixteenth-century piece can still be purchased for as little as $1,000. Their price has lagged because of small demand and large supply: few persons care to hang religious subjects in modern living rooms, and there has been a steady supply coming out of Soviet Russia.

The icon is probably one of the best investments in the art world today because Russia has finally stopped the export of icons and an increasing number are disappearing into museums. With the supply decreasing and the demand remaining steady, the price is certain to move up.

There is another area for investment where the supply is plentiful and demand has not yet developed: Oriental ancestor portraits.

In the nineteenth century it became the vogue in China to hang portraits of one's ancestors. The Chinese never considered these portraits as art—they were merely necessary signs of reverence to one's forebears—so no one "collected" them. As a result, they can be purchased today at a modest price—a few hundred dollars—despite their semi-rarity, and there is no better investment. In the past few years, with the mounting of spectacular art exhibitions like that of the Chinese treasures shown at Washington's National Gallery, Western interest in Chinese painting has increased tremendously. As relations between China and the West become "normalized," all kinds of Oriental art will be more and more in demand, and paintings of this type should be selling for more than a thousand dollars. I bought a pair painted in Shanghai in 1890 (one shown in Figure 28), and I wonder what the two elderly people in them would think if they knew that their pictures now hang in the dining room of an Occidental doctor in Toronto. In China, portraits were rarely done before the mid-

1800s or after the first quarter of the twentieth century, so they are easily dated. The best place to buy ancestor paintings is in Hong Kong, where hundreds were brought after the Chinese revolution. If you do not get a chance to visit that city, these paintings do come up for sale periodically at Parke Bernet auctions.

Watch out for as yet little-known kinds of art and artifacts, including the art of Tibet. In 1959 when the Chinese overran Tibet the head of the largest lamasery fled to India and from there emigrated to Canada. He brought with him the treasures of the lamasery, including an exquisite tea service (Figure 29). The larger cups are made of jade and the smaller of Chinese porcelain, and their covers and bases are of sterling silver overlaid with gold. I bought this set in January 1976 for $2,500—a hefty investment, it's true, but the gold and silver in the cups are worth the price alone. The lama also smuggled the entire lamasery collection of solid gold cutlery and plates into India and would like to sell them but so far the Indian government has refused to allow their export.

Tibetan art is an excellent investment today because the price is still reasonable and its innate beauty, the value of the basic materials, and its rarity are certain to draw increasing interest as this type of art becomes better known. And it will become better known. For centuries Tibet was an isolated and introverted country whose art and people remained within its mountainous boundaries; but with the communist takeover and the flight of the former ruling class, all this is changing. The Tibetan émigrés have for the most part escaped with their collections of art objects, and (following our rule about buying art after a revolution) these make an excellent investment now.

Another field well worth prospecting is that which for want of a better word I'll call celebrity painting. One example in this area is a watercolor by Henry Miller (Figure 30). He is famous for the books he wrote in the twenties in Paris for the Obelisk Press, but few people know that he is prouder of his watercolors than he is of his writings. Miller has always had an eye for beautiful women, and in 1964 he persuaded a Toronto doctor's young wife to live with him for some weeks. She arranged for me to purchase a painting—a vaguely Fauvist study of three heads—from him. Miller did not set a price on it but asked me to send him what I thought it was worth. I sent him $150.

Miller still sells his paintings for a few hundred dollars. They will surely go up in price after his death (he is over 80 now). There are many other famous amateur painters, including Churchill, Eisenhower, and Hitler. Their paintings are of historical interest and so are almost certain to prove good investments. If you get the chance to pick one up cheaply, don't let it go by.

Another recent form of art that could be classified as modern (or not antique) is that of contemporary stained glass. It has been an excellent investment—I bought a window by Angus MacDonald, one of Canada's most imaginative artists working with stained glass, in 1960 for $1,000. Today the same window would cost $5,000. But stained glass is beginning to move up rapidly in price as it becomes more and more fashionable. Associated with this increase has been a startling wave of thefts, so take care. Don't put a valuable stained glass window on an open or unguarded porch.

You can also make big profits from nonantique stone carvings made from rare *beautiful* stones, including jade found in Burma and Canada, rock crystal from Hawaii, turquoise from Turkey, Russian malachite, Armenian lapis lazuli, and so on. Jade was the first hardstone to be carved by man, and carvings done almost three thousand years ago are still in existence. (Softstone carvings from soapstone are quite a different kettle of fish. They are easily and quickly made and tend to deteriorate and break equally easily. The investor should avoid these entirely. Alas, this includes most Eskimo carvings.) A beautiful hardstone can be profitable and enjoyable for many years until you are ready to sell it to the next lucky owner.

I have a piece carved from rock crystal done in Shanghai in 1922. It was purchased in that year by a wealthy Chinese family for the equivalent of sixty U.S. dollars. In 1949 the Kuomintang government collapsed, and the son of the original purchaser fled to Taiwan, leaving his collection behind. In 1958 this carving was sold to me by the Chinese government for $650. Today similar pieces can be seen in New York galleries at prices around $10,000.

Even among antique works of art there are still types of objects that can make a good, affordable investment. I have a wooden temple carving that is several hundred years old and was taken by the Indian government from an abandoned Dravidian temple in southern India (Figure 31). In 1966, Eaton's of Toronto ran an Indian festival and

121

this was one of two ancient carvings sent to Canada along with the modern goods. Eaton's sold it for $100. Similar carvings can still be bought for about the same amount, but buyers should take care because it is difficult to distinguish modern carvings from these old pieces.

Ancient mosaics are good investments for those persons with large homes. Because of their size and weight the market for these objects is limited and as a result entire floors and walls from second-century Byzantine homes can be purchased today for the price of one automata watch—normally I would advise you to avoid them for just this reason. But how exciting it can be to walk on a floor originally laid by a Roman artist in Caesar's time! And—more to the point in a book on art investment—this is one case where you can make a limited market work to your benefit. The best mosaics in the world are to be found in Jordan; there is an ancient town called Jerash just north of Amman which is literally packed with mosaics. Visitors are told that if they wish to buy Jordanian mosaics the man to call is Jordan's Minister of Archeology! There were thousands of mosaics in north Africa, but that area has now been picked clean and the only other sources are Turkey, Iran, and occasionally Israel.

Ancient mosaics occasionally appear for sale in the United States and usually the prices are horrendous—but if you are visiting the Middle East and get the chance, do ship one home. Even if your home is too small, your museum will love to have it.

In Chapter II I advised staying clear of Judaica because of the prevalence of fakes, but there is one example of the genre that makes a truly solid investment—the marriage certificate.

Beginning in the Middle Ages and continuing right up to today it has been the custom of Jewish families to draw up a certificate for every marriage. These documents—some of them beautiful examples of calligraphy and decorative work—have begun to be eagerly sought out by both individual collectors and (most important) synagogues. The latter kind of purchaser is causing a constriction of the market, for once a piece becomes the property of an institution it is off the market forever. With the supply diminishing, demand and price have gone up. In 1967, at a Parke Bernet auction, I purchased one that was done for a marriage in Rome in 1841 (Figure 32). It cost $300; today it would be worth about $2,000. But beware—there are literally thousands of forgeries. Those that can be authenticated are sure money-makers. The simplest and cheapest method of authentication is through a visit to your local museum.

One kind of object that is a fine and virtually fake-proof investment is the antique handmade gun. In the sixteenth century, German locksmiths lovingly prepared the weapons to be used by royalty, setting beautiful patterns of ivory in wood. I have one I bought from Sotheby's in 1955 (Figure 33) for $380; today it would bring about $2,000 and is certain to continue to rise in price. This is one field where forgeries are not a problem because the art whereby these articles were manufactured by hand has been lost so forgeries are fairly obvious.

Beautiful rarities are always a good investment, and

among these the magician box is surely one of the most delightful. There were about 120 of these manufactured in the last quarter of the eighteenth century in Geneva, and they have moved up steadily but unspectacularly in price since then.

I am fortunate to have a tiny magician box that was built in a walnut shell in 1770 (Figure 34). When the magician is asked a question, a tune plays, the magician waves his wand, and the flower box opens to give the answer. It was sold at a Sotheby's auction in 1968 for $1,600.

If you ever get the chance to buy a magician box—grab it. You will never have a problem reselling it.

Snuffboxes are much more common, and those made in the eighteenth and nineteenth centuries are excellent investments, as is one of mine, made in 1783 and purchased from A La Vieille Russie in 1957 for $5,000. The box opens to reveal a complicated musical mechanism. Similar boxes sell today for about $10,000 to $15,000.

If you like this sort of thing, I strongly suggest looking into Fabergé. In the whole history of man the most beautiful jewelry ever produced was made in St. Petersburg between 1890 and 1915 in the workshops of Carl Fabergé. Fabergé turned out everything from exquisite Easter eggs for the Czar down to tiny earrings which he sold to the ordinary wealthy citizens of Russia. Fabergé is still remarkably cheap in view of its beauty and rarity, because so very much of the total is available on the American market. I bought a pair of earrings from A La Vieille Russie in New York City in 1960 for only $100.

At the beginning of February 1976 I attended the

huge Miami Antique Show and at least twenty-five or thirty of the booths were offering lovely pieces by Carl Fabergé ranging in price from just a few hundred dollars up to many thousands. There is no question that these pieces will continue to increase in price over the years. (At this show one dealer was offering the Czarina's emerald necklace for a modest $750,000.)

If the small, charming objet de vertu pleases you but Fabergé prices are a little beyond your means, form watches are beautiful, inexpensive, and available. They are an excellent place for a collector to begin.

These watches were quite common in the early part of the nineteenth century in Paris. I have two, one a mandolin watch that opens to show the time (Figure 35). This type of watch is not uncommon and rarely sells for over $1,000, and at that figure they certainly represent good value.

My other form watch is the flower type, which was very popular at the beginning of the nineteenth century. In this one the tulip opens to show the time. It can be purchased for less than $1,000.

To sum up, the way to make money buying art is to buy only beautiful objects—things that you will take pleasure in owning and will regret selling. The *big, big* profits are made by hanging on—so don't look for the quick resale. What you should be seeking is not to turn $1,000 into $2,000, but to turn $1,000 into $50,000. This happens only with very beautiful objects—for if a museum or rich collector wants some rarity and you have the only one that is available, price can become irrelevant. A perfect example is an incredible lady's pendant that was purchased from Sotheby's in 1955 (Figure 36). It dates from the mid-eighteenth century, and there is a duplicate in the British Museum. Apparently it was given as a gift to a woman prior to the collapse of the court of Louis XVI. In 1955, a Parisian dealer, Madame Aug. Seiler, sold it for $350 to a New York dealer, Mr. Barney, and he sold it to me for $1,000 some ten years later.

In November 1976 a wealthy Iranian saw it in my collection and offered to buy it, saying to me, "Set your own price." I didn't sell, even though he was willing to pay over $100,000.

X

IN CONCLUSION

The scenario I have set out in this book for making profit in art works; I know because I've done it and made a lot of money in the process. More important, I've had increasing pleasure in the process—the finding of the art, its possession, and finally its disposal. You can easily have the same pleasure and profits if you will follow my basic rules:

(1) First of all look for beautiful art objects. No matter how interesting, rare or old, any kind of art may fall out of public favor, but beauty is always sought after. And if you truly find a piece beautiful, you will feel it's worth its price in terms of the pleasure you derive from it.

(2) Old is usually better than new. If it's old there won't be any more of its type and vintage produced and it can travel freely across national boundaries without import duties.

(3) Always buy the best available of its type. The good pieces appreciate and hold their value far better than the mediocre or the slightly second-rate.

(4) As a rule it's best to avoid modern art. The exceptions are too tough to pick out.

(5) Specialize in a field that gives you pleasure.

(6) Buy small objects. They increase in value faster than larger pieces.

(7) Don't be afraid to buy objects that need repairs.

(8) Don't collect today's fad. If it hits the front pages—sell.

(9) Look for art objects wherever you travel.

(10) Seek out the debris of wars and revolutions.

(11) Frequent the dispersals of large collections owned by famous persons—or at least scrutinize the catalogs carefully.

(12) Avoid fragile objects.

(13) Avoid erotic antiques.

(14) Avoid special "limited" editions.

(15) Remember that folk art costs half or less at its point of origin. New York is not the place to buy.

(16) Usually the best place to buy is at auction.

(17) Avoid small auctions. It is safer to patronize the big three.

(18) If working through a dealer check his reputation at your local public gallery.

(19) Avoid newly discovered "old masterpieces."

(20) Learn my rules for avoiding fakes.

(21) Don't rush—take time in making your purchases.

(22) Expect to hold your pieces for a minimum of one year—better still, in the United States, hold on for six years and avoid capital gains tax.

(23) Sell your objects at auction.

And finally:

(24) Remember there is a dual purpose in buying art

for investment. Your profits will multiply many times if you buy beautiful things that give you pleasure in their company. Where else can you get enjoyment followed by profit?

INDEX